Poundbury

Poundbury

The Town that Charles Built

Dennis Hardy

Photographs by Jane Woolfenden

TCPA

Published in 2006 by
Town and Country Planning Association
17 Carlton House Terrace, London SW1Y 5AS
Website: http://www.tcpa.org.uk

British Library Cataloguing in Publication Data
A catalogue record for this book is available from the British Library

ISBN 0 902797 40 9

The TCPA is extremely grateful for the generous grant in support of the publication of this book from the Lady Margaret Paterson Osborn Trust

Printed in Great Britain by RAP Spiderweb Limited, Oldham

Contents

Foreword

The Town and Country Planning Association, with the generous support of the Lady Margaret Paterson Osborn Trust, is delighted to publish this book as part of its continuing commitment to environmental education.

Poundbury is already world famous, but people are hungry to understand how and why it was brought into being, what it feels like as a place and as a community, what future it faces, and what lessons might be drawn from it all to help us make sustainable communities elsewhere. Dennis Hardy addresses all these questions.

The TCPA has a special interest in the exciting business of building new communities. As the promoters of the idea since 1899, and as midwife to Letchworth and Welwyn Garden Cities, we quickly became the guardians of the knowledge and publicists of best practice. Our vision embodies a unique combination of separately proven ideas – that town and country, being mutually dependent, should be planned together; that the community should collectively own the land it occupies and share the benefits of its increasing value; that towns should be human in scale; that everyone, especially families, should have the choice of a decent house and garden; and that better environments are produced by planning than by sprawl. It is a challenging vision, but one which stimulates interest in all its aspects.

We have helped to persuade governments and private corporations all over the world to create new towns and major town expansion schemes where circumstances were right, and on terms that were in the public interest. Some have been wonderful, some have not. We all need continually to learn.

Poundbury is, of course, a town expansion scheme and not a new town. Its identity is so strong that it is easy to forget that it should feel fully integrated with the Dorchester of which it is part. In that sense, Poundbury is notable for itself rather than its context, a characteristic it shares with Hampstead Garden Suburb, that early spin-out from the garden city movement.

Poundbury is also a privately promoted project, rather than a government initiative, although it was evolved through proper planning processes and community consultations. The full involvement of HRH The Prince of Wales and his Duchy of Cornwall organisation can be confusing for people who are unfamiliar with our type of constitutional monarchy.

Poundbury is distinguished by a carefully considered and unusual master-plan, and by some architecture that is very distinctive. The vision is of a compact, lively mixed community with rich cultural references to continental European city-scale urbanism.

The architectural appearance of a place can easily upstage appreciation of its plan, economy, social life and biodiversity. People are easily tempted to take the architecture as the message, and forget the rest. That fate has befallen Letchworth and the elegantly composed Welwyn from time to time, and Poundbury is prone to the same superficial assessments. It is 'why, and how, and for whom' that matters, at least as much as the look of a place. A plan matters at least as much as the external appearance of the buildings that will come and go over the years, and it is the sustainability of the community and of successive waves of inhabitants which, in the end, probably matters above all else.

The Prince of Wales is to be congratulated for impelling his Duchy team to be exemplary town-builders, and to try as hard as possible to do things to the highest quality. We salute also the numerous public and private organisations and the planning authorities that have made this project possible, and the residents who are tolerant of those who come to study their Poundbury, and among whom are now many ambassadors for good town-building.

As we continue to seek appropriate forms of sustainable new development for the 21st century, it is vital that lessons are learnt from each new development. This book is a significant addition to our knowledge and shared experience. There is so much more that needs to be done in hundreds of schemes larger still and more demanding than Poundbury – but this place fuels optimism rather than pessimism in facing the future.

David Lock
Chair, Town and Country Planning Association

Preface

'Has anyone any ideas, I beg
*If this is a golden or **ersatz** egg?'*[1]

Poundbury has seldom been out of the news since the first foundations were laid in the early 1990s. In part, as the brainchild of the Prince of Wales, this level of media attention was inevitable. For more than a decade before Poundbury, the Prince had been goading leaders of the building professions with his criticism of their poor record in rebuilding Britain's cities since 1945. Modernist architects, in his eyes, were especially culpable. With his subsequent announcement of the Poundbury scheme it was 'pay back' time. Leading architects led the attack, mocking the planned experiment as little more than an exercise in fantasy; more seriously, they declared that it would never be built.

Such critics have since had to eat their words. After a slow start, held back by a sluggish property market at the time of its inception, the development of Poundbury has proceeded apace. In spite of, or more likely because of, its innovative features – such as traditional building styles, the inclusion of offices and factories, a mixing of housing tenures, and a novel road plan and virtual absence of street signage – it has become enormously popular as a place to live and work. With sustainability at the top of the national planning agenda, Poundbury is widely acclaimed as an exemplar of 21st century living, attracting numerous visitors from within Britain and overseas.

An enduring lesson, though, in a long history of model experiments in Britain is that while it is always possible to nudge towards perfection, its realisation will always be beyond reach. The evidence of Poundbury is no different. Even at this stage in its development – with more still to be built than so far completed – it has broken new ground on a variety of important fronts and its achievements should be loudly acclaimed. Yet lessons can always be learnt along the way, and some things could be done differently. More fundamentally, planners can only go so far – in the end, the most perfect environment will be peopled by the likes of us all, none of us perfect. Only if one accepts these underlying realities can a fair judgement be made.

It is at this fascinating juncture that I decided to write this book. Not often do we have such an opportunity to look at a radical experiment in the making. The story is one that deserves to be told and if only as a record of what is happening in this corner of Dorset I hope that it will fill a gap. When it comes to weighing the *pros* and *cons* of the Poundbury experiment I am sure that there will be less agreement. I have tried to present the various arguments, for and against, but in the end my own bias comes out strongly in its favour. The fact that I have chosen to live in Poundbury is itself testimony to my own predilections.

My prime aim, however, is not to impose a single view so much as to encourage a sensible debate on how we might best design new settlements for the century ahead. If we can answer the question – 'is this a golden or an *ersatz* egg?' – originally posed in the 1940s by the pioneering campaigner, Sir Frederic Osborn, in relation to a new piece of planning legislation, we might at least begin to feel more confident about how to proceed. Planners face enormous challenges in finding new ways forward and there are few enough markers along the way. Poundbury is a rare exception in telling of its own experience and it would surely be folly to ignore this.

Note
1   F.J. Osborn (1959), 'The Report of Uthwatt'

Acknowledgements

Poundbury is a story in the making, and I am deeply indebted to numerous people who have helped me to piece together the various parts.

Leon Krier is Poundbury's inspirational master-planner, and it was a great pleasure to talk to him in the relaxed ambience of his home village in the South of France. In the Duchy of Cornwall Office, I am especially grateful for the interest and advice of Simon Conibear (Poundbury Development Manager) and for the assistance of Naomi Drummond in tracing photographic records. No less am I grateful to Andrew Hamilton (Poundbury Development Director) and to David Oliver (Consultant Architect) for telling me of their own roles in helping to shape Poundbury.

Although not long in his new post as Chief Executive of The Prince's Foundation for the Built Environment, Hank Dittmar found time to meet me to discuss the importance of Poundbury as an exemplar of New Urbanism; and at the Foundation I also learnt from Ben Bolgar, Director of Design, about some of the nuances of urban coding.

Mike West, Chairman of the Residents Association, has been a constant source of advice in my dual role of local resident and author of this book; so, too, has Peter Bryant, who was an earlier Chairman of the Residents Association and has contributed in a variety of other ways too in helping to make Poundbury work. Peter Noble is another Poundbury stalwart and told me of his work as Chairman of the second of the management companies.

Philip Fry, Managing Director of the building firm C.G. Fry & Son, explained his own interest in the development, as well as how his firm has been involved from the outset. Another builder, Kim Slowe, told me of his innovative contribution that has included building an alternative health clinic and pioneering some ecologically progressive housing. Emma Coleman is a Housing Officer for the Guinness Trust and shared her own experience and sense of enthusiasm for the provision of affordable housing in Poundbury.

David Evans and Andrew Martin were both extremely open and helpful in explaining to me the role and involvement of the West Dorset District Council Planning Department. Likewise, Ian Madgwick and Dave Brown, in the Dorset County Council Highways Department, explained how highways regulations have been imaginatively adapted to meet the particular demands of Poundbury.

I am indebted to Mervyn Miller for providing me with an advance copy of his paper on Poundbury and New Urbanism, first produced for the Conference on Planning History of the Society for American City and Regional Planning History in November 2003.

Gordon and Jane Ashdown inspired me to make a visit to Seaside, where they spend several months each year, and while there I also met Phyllis Bleiweis, Executive Director of the Seaside Institute, and Stacey Brady, Seaside Director of Marketing and Public Relations. I am very grateful to them all for their various insights and for providing me with helpful literature.

As a resident of Poundbury, I have come to know many people who have not only welcomed me and my wife to this new community but have also been generous in giving time to talk about their own experiences and perceptions. Amongst the many people I have spoken to in connection with this book I am grateful for interviews with Paul, Debbie, Josh and Jordan Barney, David Barrett, Janet Bishop, Peter and Fiona Brill, Arthur and Val Cole, Isobel Hallett, Tom Johns, Tom Lane, Anna Lewis, Sue McCarthy-Moore, Angus and Ann McIntyre, Paul and Clare Newman, Roger and Jill Parmenter, Tom Parsley, and Arthur and Yvette Smith. If I have carelessly omitted anyone from this list I hope that they will forgive me.

Although most of the illustrations have been commissioned for this book, I am grateful to various individuals and organisations for enabling me to reproduce the remainder. Acknowledgements are due to Heritage Trail, Bournville Trust, New Lanark Conservation Trust, Leon Krier and the Duchy of Cornwall. In those cases where copyright has been granted by the Duchy, individual photos are attributable to Jo Lowe (pp. 51 and 52), Chris Vile (p. 109), Ian Jones (p. 147), ProPhotos (p. 155) and *Dorset Echo* (p. 163).

I have had a long involvement with the Town and Country Planning Association and was delighted when the Director, Gideon Amos, agreed to publish this book. From its inception, more than a century ago, the TCPA has promoted the benefits of new communities and it seemed only fitting to put this latest example under a critical spotlight. The skills and endless patience of Nick Matthews, who took on the role of publisher in addition to his other duties at the TCPA, have been deeply appreciated at every step in the production process.

Finally, coming to Poundbury has been an adventure for me and my wife, Jane, and when I decided to write this book it was an added pleasure that Jane agreed to take the accompanying photographs. More than that, her enthusiasm for the project and critical eye for detail has undoubtedly saved me from many a slip. Any remaining errors and omissions are, of course, my own responsibility.

Chapter 1

Cities in the Sun

'Can there ever have been a land where so many people at so many times have tried to create their ideal community?'[1]

Too often, towns and villages in Britain fail to provide a decent setting for the people who live and work in them. This was true of the past as well as now. Often places have evolved with little or no overall planning, or, worse than that, with bad plans. Nearly six decades of comprehensive town planning in Britain may have curbed the worst of what might have happened, but it has hardly created more than the odd example of a model environment. And around the world the story is generally no better.

There is, however, a rich tradition of experiments designed to create places that go well beyond the ordinary. Such experiments have relied more on wealthy philanthropists and voluntary trusts than on government agencies. Sometimes they have kept at least one foot on the ground, but in other cases their participants have been drawn into the heady world of utopia. All are fired by high ideals and a shared belief that the *status quo* is simply not good enough. One of the most influential innovators, Ebenezer Howard, founder of the garden city movement, urged his followers to take risks: 'one should never be excessively realistic in humane plans'.[2] It is unlikely that any of his fellow innovators would have disagreed with that. Poundbury, in various ways, belongs to this intriguing tradition of experiment and change – challenging convention and seeking to develop a model that could well be applied in other locations too. It is as well to start by looking at some of its precursors.

Making Models

'A clean, fresh, well-ordered house exercises on its inmates a moral no less than a physical influence, and has the direct tendency to make the members of a family sober, peaceable, and considerate of the feelings and happiness of each other.'[3]

For a generation of wealthy industrialists in the second half of the 19th century, an important motive for building model settlements was to create a happy workforce and to instil in their employees something of their own values. In viewing these experiments now it is all too easy to dismiss the efforts of Victorian philanthropists for their undoubted paternalism and missionary zeal. But to do so would ignore both the very real environmental advances they achieved, and the honourable motive of giving back something to the communities on which they built their own fortunes.

Examples of these model communities are quite widespread but in some areas they were more concentrated than in others. The West Riding of Yorkshire – especially in the area of Bradford and Halifax – proved to be fertile ground for such ventures. This concentration was not coincidental, for the leading players were closely associated and had much in common. Sir Titus Salt (founder of Saltaire), Colonel Akroyd (Copley and Akroydon) and the Crossley family (West Hill Park district of Halifax) were all wealthy industrialists with family and business links with each other, had each held office as Lord Mayor of Bradford or Halifax, and were all staunch Congregationalists.

Sir Titus Salt's project, although larger in scale than most, typifies the spirit of this kind of experiment. His great wealth was founded in Bradford on the import of alpaca for the manufacture of worsted. The story goes that he was inspired by a reading of Benjamin Disraeli's *Sybil*, in which a model mill village is contrasted with an impoverished, unplanned community. Either way, in 1850, he commissioned a Bradford firm of architects, Lockwood and Mawson, to realise his dream of building what came to be known as Saltaire.

Saltaire: Titus Salt's mill (Courtesy: Heritage Trail)

A site was chosen a few miles from Bradford, on the banks of the River Aire, with good rail and canal links. The mill was to be the centrepiece of the new settlement, a massive structure as large as St Paul's Cathedral, and boldly presented in an Italianate style. No less grand were some of the other public buildings, not least of all the Congregational church, described by a contemporary, Abraham Holroyd, as 'the most exquisite example of pure Italian architecture in the kingdom'. As well as this church there were also sites for other denominations, as well as for baths and wash-houses, day schools and a Sunday school, almshouses and an infirmary, the Saltaire Club and Institute, and across the river a very fine public park.

Although they followed a traditional grid layout, the 850 houses for his workers were built to a higher standard than was usual at that time. Most of the houses had three bedrooms (an advance on the typical industrial 'two up and two down'), and each household enjoyed its own private yard and outside privy and fuel store. Space to the front and rear ensured that they were well ventilated, in contrast to the damp and dingy cellars and back-to-back housing in neighbouring towns.

It was in every sense a model Victorian community, yet what distinguished it from the commonplace was less its auspicious architecture than the paternalism of Salt himself. The building of Saltaire was for him a means not simply to provide a better physical environment but also to improve moral standards and social behaviour. Salvation, education and sanitation were the watchwords, and no effort was spared to save souls, extend intellectual boundaries and cleanse bodies. He was a devoted Congregationalist but encouraged other places of worship as well, in the belief that it was his 'duty and a privilege to co-operate with Christians of all evangelical denominations in furtherance of Christian work'.[4] In front of the school buildings were two lions, symbolising Vigilance and Determination, facing an identical pair, War and Peace, in front of the Institute. The lions were supposedly destined for the pedestals at the foot of Nelson's Column in Trafalgar Square, but Salt acquired them instead. Public houses were prohibited – 'drink and lust are at the bottom of it all', he once declared – and drinking and swearing was forbidden in the public park. A dim view was taken of untidy lines of washing hung in the yards, and residents were encouraged to use the wash-houses.

Saltaire was a model of its kind but by no means unique, whether in Yorkshire or in other parts of the country. Gillian Darley's book, *Villages of Vision*, remains the definitive guide to this fascinating world of philanthropic planning.[5] She points to many examples of country estate villages built by landowners, as well as to industrial ventures, typically blending morals with good housing, religion with industriousness. Towards the end of the 19th century she can point also to more ambitious schemes that took an altogether more progressive look at the potential of town planning. Port Sunlight, on Merseyside, and Bournville, in the West Midlands, were the best known and most influential of this new generation of model settlements.

The Merseyside community (dating from the late 1880s) was based on the fortunes of a soap manufacturer, W.H. Lever, who wanted to go beyond the mere provision of model housing for his workers. The whole emphasis was on

Port Sunlight: village post office

Bournville: Linden Road and post office

creating a healthy and fulfilling environment, far superior to the barren settlements elsewhere in the region. Like most such providers Lever himself was a religious man, a non-conformist, who saw it as his mission to 'socialise and Christianise business relations'.[6]

Port Sunlight evolved as an industrial village, with an exceptional range of social and cultural facilities, all kept out of sight and sound of the large factory on which the whole enterprise was founded. House styles were varied, drawing on the half-timbered patterns of vernacular Cheshire architecture as well as displaying a romantic flair in the use of high Flemish gables. Gardens and allotments were generous and trees were planted along the broad avenues, and the wide range of social facilities included (unusually for a philanthropic venture) a licensed inn. Of special note, too, was an art gallery, designed as a small Renaissance temple and set in formal gardens, dedicated by Lever to the memory of his wife. Like other progressive thinkers in that period, Lever believed that a common disinterest in art was a reflection of lack of opportunity rather than anything inherent and that an easily accessible facility of this sort would awaken dormant interest.

There was much on offer in the community but critics also pointed to a price to pay for its residents, who were eternally indebted to the community's founder; in the words of one trade union official, 'no man of an independent turn of mind could breathe for long in the atmosphere of Port Sunlight'.[7]

In spite of reservations in some quarters, the overwhelming response to Port Sunlight was very positive. From the outset it attracted admiring visitors from Britain and overseas, being seen along with Bournville as a promising model for the future. Its popular appeal even led to it featuring as the setting for a stage musical, *The Sunshine Girl*. It remains to this day a distinctive if not contradictory place, described by one contemporary observer as 'a startling place to visit, something like a film set, depicting a Platonic type of country life, leafy and leisurely but far too self-conscious for comfort'.[8] When the travel writer Bill Bryson visited Port Sunlight in search of the quirkiness of the country he had adopted as his second home he was pleasantly surprised to discover 'a proper little garden community, and much cheerier than the huddled stone cottages of Saltaire'.[9]

Often linked with Port Sunlight as another example of progressive philanthropy, Bournville (started in 1895) was the brainchild of the chocolate manufacturer George Cadbury. Like other leading chocolate families (notably, the Frys of Bristol and the Rowntrees of York), the Cadburys were devout Quakers and members of all three families saw it as their moral duty to return

George Cadbury: founder of Bournville (Courtesy: Bournville Trust)

to their workforce some of the benefits that they had themselves accrued. Working with the architect W. Alexander Harvey, Cadbury (like Lever at Port Sunlight) conceived Bournville from the outset as more than improved housing for his workers. His vision was for a total community in a garden setting. Whereas Saltaire replicated the geometrical layout that was commonplace in industrial towns at that time, and even Port Sunlight was relatively compact, Bournville broke new ground with its generous gardens and tree-lined roads. In the centre of the village was a large green with shops and other facilities alongside. And around the main factory were colourful rose gardens where the workers could relax in their breaks.

Housing was built cheaply and offered at rents that workers could afford. Yet, in spite of their cheapness, tenants found themselves in conditions of a far higher standard than most had known before. Even the smallest cottages had three bedrooms, and all were provided with a gas cooker and fitted cupboards. There were outhouses for coal and tools, a washing line and an outside lavatory (considered more hygienic than indoors) for each family. The large garden plots were all prepared for the first tenants with paths and a lawn as well as a small orchard.

Time had moved on from Saltaire, and Cadbury (even more so than Lever) was less paternalistic than mid-Victorian Salt; many of the residents at Bournville, for instance, were not Cadbury employees, and there was a less obvious expectation that everyone in the community would attend church. But in other respects he had his own ideas; there were no licensed premises within the village, physical exercise was encouraged and there was training in gardening and horticulture. Growing one's own produce would, Cadbury believed, not only lead, desirably, to a more vegetarian diet but might also encourage greater self-dependence. Bournville attracted visitors from far and wide and was compared very favourably with the overcrowded, smoky conditions in nearby Birmingham. People who lived in Cadbury's settlement were shown to be healthier than those in neighbouring industrial towns, and the 'garden village' idea was to have enormous influence on later developments elsewhere.

Leafy suburbs were coming into vogue but there were also variations on the earlier theme; in particular, some model developments deliberately excluded places of employment. A pioneering exemplar in West London was the garden suburb of Bedford Park (dating from 1877), planned from the outset by Jonathan Carr as a dormitory suburb just half an hour from the City. It was an extravagant and colourful scheme that attracted notable Arts and Crafts architects of the day, and the new houses were marketed complete with William Morris wallpapers. The housing was solid and detached, with popular features such as verandahs and conservatories, and generous gardens and avenues well planted with trees. Bedford Park appealed especially to middle-class Bohemians, and the early residents included a good representation of artists and authors, architects and playwrights. The self-conscious village community they created drew mischievous criticism from outsiders, as in the following verse that appeared in a copy of the *St James Gazette* in 1881:

'Thus was a village builded
For all who are aesthete
Whose precious souls it fill did
With utter joy complete.'

A quarter of a century later, Hampstead Garden Suburb would also in time become something of an intellectual's retreat, but the difference there was that its founder, Dame Henrietta Barnett, started with loftier ideals of social integration. Henrietta Barnett had previously worked with her husband, Canon Barnett, in the university settlement Toynbee Hall, which he had established in London's East End, genuinely believing that bringing the classes together would be of benefit to all. Hampstead Garden Suburb was the setting

Queen Mary and Dame Henrietta Barnett (centre) viewing Hampstead Garden Suburb: the interest of royalty in experimental communities is clearly nothing new

for her experiment and her choice of the socialist architect Raymond Unwin to plan the development was well considered. Unwin shared his sponsor's idealism, and the site, with all the advantages of looking onto Hampstead Heath coupled with proximity to Golders Green station and easy access to the City, was perfect for the purpose. The garden suburb emerged with all the trappings of a romantic set-piece – winding roads and picturesque cottages, village greens and indigenous hedgerows – and it was widely acknowledged as a very desirable place to live. But the intended social engineering was less successful and even the founder, some 20 years after its inception, questioned whether 'enough of the residents make real attempts to know intimately the classes which do not belong socially to their own'.[10]

Garden City Utopia

'Town and country must be married, and out of this joyous union will spring a new hope, a new life, a new civilisation.'[11]

Garden villages or garden suburbs were one thing, but for the social reformer Ebenezer Howard they could never really lead to essential change; they had already proved themselves as better living environments than the norm of industrial towns and cities but they were inevitably cast – and thereby limited – in the philanthropic (or even commercial) mould of their founders. Instead, Howard, an inventor by nature and shorthand clerk by trade, wanted to cast the net much wider, to bring about social change. He was certainly not a violent revolutionary – far from it as his whole approach was based on gentle persuasion – but in his own way he wanted to see many of society's ills put to right. The title of his seminal book (published in 1898), *To-Morrow: A Peaceful Path to Real Reform*, set the tone for his ambitious intentions.

Howard, whose ideas were to have a lasting impact on developments in the 20th century, was an unlikely instigator of radical change. Born into a lower middle-class household in London in 1850, there was nothing in his early career to suggest future fame. He drifted from school into the mundane world of City of London clerks, where he worked for a few years before impulsively leaving to seek his fortune in the United States. There were romantic dreams of making a living on the land but the hard reality of manual labour soon forced him back to city life, this time to Chicago, where he picked up his original career as a shorthand writer for a legal firm. America was a land

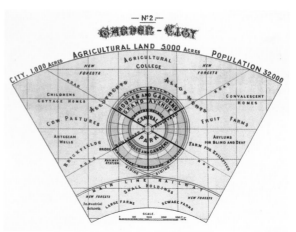

Above: Diagram of a garden city (from Howard's original book)

Left: Ebenezer Howard

of ideas and when Howard returned to London in 1876 he brought back with him a belief in his own mission to improve the lot of mankind. For someone with a social agenda, his new job of recording events in the House of Commons was an appropriate setting, while outside his work he attended lectures and meetings to hear some of the political and intellectual leaders of the day. Gradually, his ideas started to focus around the formation of what he termed the 'garden city', his building block for a new society.

It was more than 20 years, though, before he produced (with the help of a loan from an American friend) his modestly presented book, sold initially for one shilling a copy. Nor was its reception necessarily a sign of things to come – a mixture of qualified enthusiasm and outright rejection as just another utopian scheme that would go the way of all the others. Howard himself was not to be deterred and, convinced of its potential, in the following year, 1899, a new organisation was formed, the Garden City Association, to promote his ideas and to initiate the world's first garden city.

In Howard's view, there were drawbacks to both urban and rural life yet also attractions. Towns, for instance, were unhealthy, crowded, noisy and dangerous, but at the same time stimulating, with plenty of jobs and places to visit. In turn, the countryside offered little employment opportunity, housing was poor and wages were low, but it was peaceful, healthy and with well-established communities. His solution was for a hybrid, taking the best of town and country to produce the garden city. Moreover, he believed that the very creation of garden cities would lead to the progressive decline of large urban concentrations like London, as firms and individuals chose to leave behind high rents and poor housing in favour of this brave new world in the countryside, *urbs in rure*.

In *To-Morrow*, Howard set out in detail how it would all work. The new settlement was to be a city in a garden, as well as a city of gardens, designed for an ultimate population of 30,000 with another 2,000 in a surrounding agricultural belt. It is shown on his plan as a circular settlement, with concentric avenues and in the centre an ornamental park surrounded by civic buildings. Shops would be located in a Crystal Palace, a wide glass arcade with shops and exhibitions. The outer limits of the garden city were to be defined by an agricultural belt.

The unique feature of Howard's scheme, however, lay less in the careful layout and more in the pattern of ownership. Investors would receive a fair return for their capital but land and development would be vested in the common ownership of a Trust. All occupants would pay a rent to the Trust, to be used to repay the initial investors and to fund general running costs and welfare facilities. Howard's premise was that once the capital costs were repaid the community as a whole would benefit from receiving a higher proportion of the rental income, coupled with the gains resulting from rising land values. Garden cities would, therefore, enjoy a better provision of amenities than other towns, a prediction that has, in fact, been more than amply borne out in the experience of Letchworth, the first garden city.

With the support of wealthy, liberal-minded businessmen, land was bought for the venture, the site of what was soon to become Letchworth. Additional capital was raised to build it, and the young architects Raymond Unwin and Barry Parker were commissioned to prepare the overall plan and to influence the design of individual buildings. Their own pedigree was impeccable for the task, steeped in an Arts and Crafts tradition and with strong sympathies for a very English brand of socialism; over Unwin's desk were portraits of Edward Carpenter and William Morris.

In spite of its innovative pedigree, most of the new garden city proved to be, in one sense, quite conventional by present standards; it marked a material improvement, however, in the quality of the everyday environment of its inhabitants. Under the influence of Unwin and Parker, houses were designed in a picturesque, vernacular style, based on that of 16th- and 17th-century cottages. Typically, they would have steeply-sloping red tile roofs, with gables and dormer windows, and white or cream roughcast elevations; and they would be grouped, often in terraces of four, along tree-lined avenues or around village greens. Important architects of the day were invited to design some of the larger houses (the aim being to attract residents from all classes), which tended to follow the style set by Unwin and Parker. Every dwelling had its own garden, and the architects were careful to ensure that as far as possible natural features in the landscape were preserved. As a result, visitors were invariably impressed by the verdant appearance of the town and by the profusion of flowers.

There was a conscious attempt to ensure that a reasonable proportion of new housing would be available at low prices. Unwin and Parker designed four-roomed cottages for as little as £132, but were less than enthusiastic for a commercially sponsored competition which invited architects to produce their own designs and to build demonstration cottages for less than £150. Although this exercise, the Cheap Cottages Competition and Exhibition, attracted considerable interest, the feeling was that it led to a dilution of the dominant style and that some cost-cutting was achieved only at the expense of a lowering of standards.

Separated from the housing, industrial development made good progress in the early years. Firms were attracted to Letchworth, not necessarily by the radical principles that Howard first expounded (although the owners of some who moved, like the Idris Mineral Water Works, and the publisher, Dent, were more than sympathetic), but probably more often by the practical advantages of serviced sites with good communications and a ready supply of labour. Much to the dismay of those, not least of all women, who looked to Letchworth for a break from past conventions, the most prominent factory in the early days was that of the Spirella Corset Company.

Typically, however, it was less the evidence of solid achievement in creating a high-quality environment with local employment that attracted most interest amongst observers, but rather that which was seen as quirky and eccentric. In spite of the acceptance of Howard's ideas by respectable businessmen, the garden city never lost its more challenging, utopian associations in the minds of critics and supporters alike. And in its way these associations became self-fulfilling, with those espousing alternative lifestyles finding their way to the pioneer settlement and encouraging others to join them. Letchworth thus became something of a crossroads for free-thinkers, on a perpetual journey to and from the various points on the utopian map of England: for here, as one of the garden city pioneers himself observed, 'a town was to be built that would, they thought, change the face of England'.[12]

There had been many false dawns amongst the community experiments of the previous century, but Letchworth inspired new optimism, with the prospect of 'a Utopia of clean, pure air, flowers and perpetual sunshine'.[13] Tolstoyans, Ruskinian socialists, and members of the Independent Labour Party were amongst those who made their home in the garden city. To outsiders they seemed an odd set: 'a typical citizen clad in knickerbockers and, of course, sandals, a vegetarian and member of the Theosophical Society who kept two tortoises which he polishes regularly with the best Lucca oil. Over his mantelpiece was a large photo of Madame Blatavsky and on his library shelves were *Isis Unveiled* and the works of William Morris, H.G. Wells and Tolstoy.'[14]

Jan Marsh has shown how a popular neighbourhood for these free-thinkers was in the south-west of the town, in a cluster of more expensive cottages. She cites a contemporary view that those who settled there were the 'enthusiasts who had been looking forward for years to the founding of the town. They came to it in a spirit of adventure, they discovered it as if it were a new land.'[15]

Mervyn Miller, author of the seminal book on Letchworth, agrees that before 1914 there was something special about the place, 'a Golden Age of Garden City life'.[16] In that period it acquired a reputation for 'smocks, sandals

Letchworth: from the outset, critics drew attention to the 'bohemianism' of the first settlers

and, in the context of highly conventional moral standards of the day, scandals'.[17] Miller is also careful to point out that, in spite of this reputation, the free-thinkers were always very much in a minority – 'almost universally middle class, the successors of the Utopianists of earlier centuries'[18] – and most of the town got on with its business much as in any other place.

In spite of their minority status, the free-thinkers exercised a disproportionate influence on the cultural life of Letchworth in its early days, with a predictable diet of 'improving' lectures, craft-making, revival of traditional music and dance, and educational experiments. High-minded pioneers supported a temperance policy, conviviality in the Skittles Inn was fuelled by nothing stronger than cocoa and fruit cordials, and vegetarianism was widely practiced. For those who wished to, there were opportunities for co-operative living, with its offer of a mixture of private accommodation and shared facilities, including kitchens, dining rooms and gardens. Howard wrote in 1913 of Letchworth's first co-operative project, 'Homesgarth', designed by the Fabian architect J. Clapham Lander, with accommodation for 30 'happy people' – mainly of the middle class, he conceded, but it was his 'great ambition to carry out a similar scheme which will benefit the people of the working class'.[19]

Even without the more exotic features of the new settlement, Letchworth was a pioneering project and attracted a regular stream of international as well as domestic visitors. In the summer of 1905, for instance, 60,000 people were attracted to the Cheap Cottages Exhibition. Recognising the propagandist value of the new settlement, the Garden City Association was active in arranging its own visits and in publicising progress in other ways; its periodical, *The Garden City*, for instance, carried monthly notes and articles on this. Additionally (and largely as a result of the work of the Secretary, Thomas Adams) the Garden City Company played its own part in the process. Adams organised a diverse programme of visits, hosting such groups as adult education bodies, cyclists, women Liberals, vegetarians, the Christian Social Union, and MPs from all parties.

On balance, the response of visitors appears to have been favourable. Some grumbled about the mud, and the half-finished state of it all, but most saw beyond the short-term difficulties. After all, here – in contrast with the harsh reality of conventional urbanism – was evidence of well-designed housing in a healthy environment, with local employment, accessible to working people as well as being attractive for these and other reasons to middle-class residents. Whether or not it was, in a literal sense, utopian would have mattered little to those who personally experienced a dramatically improved environment. 'You are going nowhere better', said one pioneer to those who were foolish enough to pass the town by.

Even George Bernard Shaw, not one to give praise lightly, was in 1904 prepared to commend (in his play *John Bull's Other Island*) the building of a garden city in Ireland, and a copy of Howard's book is handed on the stage from one actor to another; while in the following year, in *Major Barbara*, Letchworth is featured in the guise of Perivale St. Andrews, 'a spotlessly clean and beautiful hillside town'.

By 1914 some 10,000 people lived in the garden city, and this alone was no mean achievement when compared with the many earlier model schemes that had never progressed beyond the printed word. In other respects, though, Letchworth fell short of utopian ideals. Conditions might have been improved for its workers, but the basic infrastructure of capitalist society remained untouched. Moreover, even on its own terms, the garden city on the ground had lost something of Howard's original ideals. In an internal Garden City Association memorandum, it was shown that there were shortfalls between theory and practice in relation to methods of raising capital, administration, ownership of the sites and public services, land tenure, the size of the estate, the proportion reserved for agriculture, restrictions on growth, layout, and the system of distribution. Some of the reasons for these differences were purely pragmatic (depending, for instance, on the extent and configuration of the estate) but there was also a tendency to adopt a more commercial approach than had been originally intended. The fact is that Letchworth was, not surprisingly, a reformist rather than a revolutionary project, with its own strengths as well as weaknesses. This positioning was noted in an article in *The Race-Builder*: 'The revolutionist may regard it as a last ditch for the hard-pressed forces of capitalism, but the evolutionists should surely see it as an effort to find a way out of the competitive chaos towards a well-ordered society. If the scheme retains some old evils, it introduces new qualifying virtues.'[20]

Similarly, it has been noted how the loss of some of its idealistic elements widened its appeal: 'The green banner of the garden city became respectable and the sharp Utopian outlines of Howard's sketches softened and blurred.'[21]

Paradoxically, in spite of its obvious reformist qualities, there were at the same time those who condemned Letchworth for being fanciful, diversionary and irrelevant to the real needs of the country; in short, for being utopian. Such critics were less interested in the solid achievements of Letchworth and more in the extremism of a minority. They were quick to jeer at the 'cranks' in the town, pouring scorn on the wearing of smocks and djibbahs, on the making of their own sandals, on the vegetarian and non-alcoholic régime, and on the long hair and beards. They found an easy butt for their ridicule in the plain fare of the Food Reform Restaurant and the prospects of a stay at the Simple Life Hotel.

Some of the cartoons and press articles were merely humorous but sometimes they revealed a note of spite, if not fear of potentially subversive effects on society. In *Mr Standfast*, John Buchan sent his First World War hero Richard Hannay *incognito* to Bigglewick (Letchworth by another name) in search of dissidents. Our hero is quick to discover that most of them are

Letchworth: poster issued by First Garden City Limited (c. 1925)

pacifists, but apart from being 'the rummiest birds you can imagine' generally harmless. At worst they were misguided: 'about half were respectable citizens who came here for country air and low rates, but even these had a touch of queerness'. Some years later, George Orwell, in *The Road to Wigan Pier*, used the popular view of Letchworth to support his broadside on what he saw as the 'cranky' side of socialism; in the garden city, he claimed, one could find 'every fruit juice drinker, sandal wearer, sex-maniac, Quaker, nature cure quack, pacifist and feminist in England'.

Letchworth, disliked by some for not going far enough and by others for being too utopian, was caught in a cleft stick of criticism. But on the ground it continued to grow, and although Howard's rational path to a world of garden cities was not universally or quickly followed, the experience gained was nevertheless to have some consequential effects. Welwyn, another site in Hertfordshire, was to be the location of the only other garden city of its kind.

After that, Britain was to put its trust in the State, in preference to eccentric individuals like Howard and the profit-seeking private sector. After the Second World War new legislation was passed and development corporations were formed to manage an ambitious programme of new towns.

Not until the 1960s were there modest signs of a return of privately sponsored schemes, the most enduring being New Ash Green in Kent. The aim there was to create a balanced community in a wooded environment in Kent, modelled on a distinctive Scandinavian style of architecture. Just three years after its inception, the original developer – a small firm of architects and planners – was forced into bankruptcy and the scheme was completed on more conventional lines by one of the major building companies. The depressing conclusion voiced by one observer was that 'it is not possible to build good housing and make money'.[22]

In spite of the omens from New Ash Green, the 1980s saw a number of new initiatives for model villages, promoted by a consortium of the largest building companies. The consortium enjoyed weighty financial backing and a political climate that favoured private enterprise, yet none of its proposals was to see the light of day, in most cases snuffed at birth by local objections to new development on greenfield sites.[23]

Even this salutary experience has not dimmed an enduring enthusiasm to create new settlements broadly along garden city lines. In this first decade of the 21st century – with the celebration of Letchworth's centenary now past – there are renewed efforts to demonstrate the relevance of the original principles to contemporary needs, and to find a form of garden city that can be used to meet current challenges in housing and planning.[24]

New Jerusalems

'Where dawns, with hope serene, a brighter day
Than e'er saw Albion in her happiest times.' [25]

More radical certainly than model villages and even garden cities is a history of ventures that truly sought to turn the world upside down. These were visions of places in the sun, of cities on a mystical hill. There were no half measures with these: a mirror was held up to reveal the frailties of society as it was and plans were laid to rebuild it in a re-cast image. New communities were the building blocks for this Albion resurgent.

New Lanark: 1818
watercolour showing the
industrial village where
Robert Owen made some
of his first experiments
(Courtesy: New Lanark
Conservation Trust)

One of the most colourful episodes took place nearly two centuries ago in the early decades of the 19th century, under the banner of utopian socialism. And the name most closely associated with that era is Robert Owen, gamekeeper turned poacher in making the transition from mill-owner to socialist pioneer. For Owen, it was not the new industrialisation that threatened human happiness but the capitalist form of organisation; too much wealth found its way into the hands of a few at the expense of the many who worked to create it for a pittance in the mines and factories. A new form of education was the key to opening people's minds to the potential of a more rational society, and Owen is recalled for some important experiments on that front. But in his wider scheme he believed that the most appropriate unit of organisation for the many changes he envisaged would be in the form of communities of a couple of thousand people. These would be on a meaningful human scale and would contain places of work as well as recreation.

He first made some practical and well-received changes to the environment of his mill village New Lanark, in Scotland, but soon came up against the resistance of his business partners concerned more about their profits, and local dignitaries who feared the spread of Owen's upstart ideas. Rebuffed in this way he cut his ties completely with the Establishment and designed a scheme for fully-fledged socialist communities. As well as inspiring others to do the same, he personally supported a number of different experiments, in Britain and the United States. At one stage he even gained an audience with the then American President to present a three-dimensional model of his ideal community, recommending it as a prototype for the future settlement of the whole of the young nation.

At Harmony Hall in Hampshire, between 1839 and 1845, Owen used what was left of his own wealth to create a model socialist community. No expense was spared to build a magnificent mansion to accommodate the socialists who were drawn to the experiment. Symbolically, above the front door porch the letters 'CM' were carved to denote that all who entered would experience the 'commencement of the millennium'. Instead of simplicity, the interior was lavish, not only in terms of its fittings but also with elaborate equipment that was intended to illustrate the powers of science in a rational society. A miniature train carried dishes between the dining room and kitchen.

But the whole thing was too elaborate, and an honest attempt to apply socialist principles was soon to disintegrate. Owen himself flitted in and out as he tried at the same time to keep alive other ventures too, while the location of Harmony Hall in rural Hampshire was never the best part of the country in which to engage with other arms of the socialist movement. More fundamentally, the change that was expected of the pioneers in abandoning overnight familiar ways in favour of revolutionary change was altogether too much. Critics were quick to point out these inevitable failings, as illustrated in the following verse:

'Oh, Socialism is a pretty thing
For bards to sing:
And Harmony's a title worth some guineas,
To take in ninnies...'[26]

Undeterred by the eventual collapse of each of the utopian socialist communities, other visionaries with different combinations of ideas set about their own attempts to create communities as vanguards of the new life. This was to be especially so in the United States, where the very idea of the 'land of the free' was sufficient to entice thousands of adventurers from the Old World to plant their own exotic hybrids of political, religious and artistic utopias. Even the very act of turning one's back on the old, corrupt institutions of Europe and of crossing the Atlantic was seen as a symbolic transition between old and new, imperfect and perfect.

Meanwhile, in Britain, although less numerous than their American counterparts, new communities were formed for a similar variety of reasons. Feargus O'Connor, the Chartist leader, veered away from his failed political movement in the 1840s to initiate an extraordinary scheme to settle industrial workers on the land. O'Connor believed that, in becoming landowners, not only would working people gain a political vote (otherwise denied to them) but the very act of managing a small plot of land would foster a new sense of self-assurance. Five villages were built and settled, including the eponymous O'Connorville, now on the western fringe of London. For other visionaries, religion rather than politics was the driving force, and small communities were envisaged as refuges where the chosen few would await salvation. Yet again, some were inspired by anarchist ideas (including those of Leo Tolstoy), with community as the obvious unit of organisation in place of geographical and political centres of power.

The utopian tradition is in one sense remarkably consistent, with experiments arising at all times in history; in another sense, though, the nature of these experiments differs markedly, depending on the time and place of their conception. New problems arise at different times and it is the job of utopians to find ways around these. Thus, in the early 20th century, the Arts and Crafts architect C.R. Ashbee, in his endeavour to revive craft production, organised the wholesale migration of craftsmen and their families from workshops in Whitechapel, East London, to establish a colony in the Cotswolds. 'The proper place for the Arts and Crafts is in the country, the place where the children ought to be, in among the direct, elemental facts of life, and away from the complex, artificial and often destructive influences of machinery and the great towns... the Arts and Crafts must go *back to the land.'*[27] Ashbee's was a radical experiment that addressed some of the wider concerns of the time.

After a period of reconnaissance, Ashbee selected the sleepy little town of Chipping Campden for his experiment. About 50 craftsmen and their families (some 150 people in total) made the journey from East London, arriving in stages between May and August 1902 according to their different workshop affiliations. First came the wood shop and its members, then the forge and metal shop; the Essex House Press was the last to be installed. Overall, it was a sizeable migration – of plant and materials as well as people – and 150 newcomers represented a significant proportion of the town's 1500 existing residents. Little wonder that Ashbee reflected, with more than a hint of mischief, that 'it will be interesting to watch the result of the impact of the Cockney upon this little decaying town'.[28]

For the focus of the enterprise, Ashbee chose a former silk mill, built on three floors in traditional stone, and set in an acre and a half of gardens with an orchard; it was renamed Essex House for this new phase in its history. On the ground floor went the Essex House Press, together with a showroom, drawing office and administration, with jewellery, silver and enamelling on

Chipping Campden: location for C.R. Ashbee's community of 'Cockneys in the country'

the first floor, and cabinet making, woodcarving and French polishing above. The blacksmiths were located in an outhouse. The main building was fitted with electricity (the first in the town to be so), so that it could be well lit throughout long working days. Machinery was used sparingly and the different crafts were organised around a common creed: in Ashbee's words, 'with the object of making useful things, of making them well and of making them beautiful'.[29]

Impressions were invariably favourable. One contemporary visitor typically observed that they had created an idyllic working environment: 'every window looks on to a common garden, every bench has a posy on it. Nothing could be more delightful than to be doing rationally good work in such surroundings.'[30] Those who had read William Morris's utopian romance, *News from Nowhere,* would also have seen a likeness to Morris's vision of future production, organised in 'banded workshops … that is, places where people collect who want to work together … to do hand-work in which working together is necessary or convenient; such work is often very pleasant'.[31]

As part of the complete tapestry of pre-industrial craft revival, Ashbee also sought to restore something of the town's cultural traditions, with folk dancing in the main square and gardening classes. There was a parallel attempt to increase education opportunities and places for recreation. His vision was for the craft colony to be a hub in a wider web of activities that would see the renaissance of the town as a whole. It was a grand vision, yet in little more than six years Ashbee had to withdraw his support. For all the quality of production that was at the heart of the colony's economy, it proved impossible to compete with more mechanised methods and the practice of stores like Liberty's that bought on the basis of price rather than whether or not something was made by hand. Ashbee's dream was not to be, although a number of the colonists stayed on in the district to pursue their individual skills and to endow Chipping Campden, to the present day, with a rich tradition of craft production and shops.

Ashbee's bold enterprise in marrying community with art was unique, although later artists were to experiment in their own way. Many, for instance, preferred the idea of a loose network of contacts and shared interests rather than a tightly formed community. In Cornwall, artists gathered at Newlyn and St Ives in colonies rather than communities. In contrast, the artist Eric Gill favoured a tighter structure and tried several times (between 1908 and the time of his death in 1940) to create his communitarian ideal of combining art with a concentrated mix of Catholic principles; for him 'small communities are not only much to be encouraged, but are the only hope'.[32] First at Ditchling in Sussex, then to the remote site of Capel-y-ffin in the Welsh Black Mountains, and finally closer to London, at Piggotts in the Chilterns, Gill gathered around him his family and close associates in an attempt to attain spiritual as well as artistic perfection. But, while he built his own reputation, in each case his community aims proved to be beyond him. There was always something contradictory in Gill's idealisation of a monastic existence and the excesses of his personal behaviour, a contradiction that cut sharply through the very notion of a community.

Probably the most successful of all such experiments was Dartington, a comprehensive rural revival community in idyllic countryside in the heart of Devon. The estate was bought in 1925, following the marriage of the sponsors, Leonard and Dorothy Elmhirst, and (with the help of Dorothy's American based fortune) the many-sided community was carefully honed in response to their own ideals. Over the years, Dartington was to be a significant

Dartington: boys from the progressive school worked on the land as part of their rounded education

development, with an enduring reputation for innovation in education, arts and crafts, organic production on the land and support for rural industries. It was always, though, to be more than a series of disjointed enterprises, for running through the whole venture was an underlying sense of spirituality and a belief that in a troubled world good would win through. There was an undying faith in the worth of the experiment and, in Dorothy's words, 'in our dream of the good life we counted on human values of kindness and friendship to bind the community together'.[33]

On a utopian map of Britain, Dartington is one of the unquestionable landmarks, not least of all because it continues today as a place of innovation and is accessible to the public. The school closed in 1987 (its very progressiveness eventually undermining its economic viability) but other features flourish. Education retains a prominent role, notably in the Dartington College of Arts and in the more recent Schumacher College, an international centre for ecological studies named after the proponent of the idea that 'small is beautiful'. Visitors flock each year to the craft workshops and to buy the famous Dartington products, and to attend some of the regular public performances and events. The manor (originally the home of the school) has been converted for conference use, and its immediate grounds are maintained to exceptionally high standards that attract a regular flow of 'garden tourists'. Further afield on the estate, the farmland and woods are carefully tended as commercial operations, but always with a sensitive eye for ecological balance. In some respects, Dartington is more successful now than in its early years; more in tune with a contemporary concern for environmental sustainability and more accessible to outsiders.

Throughout the first half of the 20th century, community experiments were driven by high ideals and a common desire to create a way through the bleak landscape of two world wars, the threat of totalitarianism abroad, high unemployment in the 1930s, and a seeming collapse of humane values. In different and often ingenious ways the searchers for utopia sought islands in a turbulent sea. Understandably, pacifism was a potent source of effort and, especially in the late 1930s and during the Second World War there were numerous groups who espoused pacifist values and who worked on the land in preference to engaging in military action. Religious beliefs, whether or not linked to the pacifist cause, were also a constant reason for community formation. Nothing illustrates this better than a revival of the quintessential community, the monastery, which found new life in the early 20th century. There were various examples, but Buckfast Abbey (just a few miles from

Buckfast Abbey: the resident monks were directly responsible for the revival of the monastic community

Dartington) is legendary, for here a few monks rebuilt the ancient abbey with their own hands and created a flourishing community. Like Dartington, this has gone from strength to strength and is a popular venue for visitors in search of spiritual inspiration as well as the heritage interest of the site.

Later in the century, as part of the great outwash of the 1960s, this search for perfection took a different form, led then by a younger generation that had become impatient with the old conventions. They, in their own way, turned the world upside down in favour of often anarchic communes, questioning everything that had previously been taken for granted. Their very radicalism led quickly to the demise of some, but other communes have managed to survive now for several decades. Modern communitarians speak of greening the cities and restoring the land, of turning back the tide of traffic and making good housing available to all, of a world of peace and equity for the many nations that struggle relentlessly against poverty. Their message has a current ring but in so many ways they inherit a lengthy tradition of comparable experiment and an unwillingness to accept things as they are.

If this is a long introduction it is because the case needs to be made that Poundbury has not arisen in a vacuum. It is, instead, a modern experiment that inherits elements, in different ways, from a lengthy and varied tradition of innovation. We will see in the following pages that Poundbury does not purport to change the world; yet even to seek to change a small part sets it aside from the commonplace. There are high ideals at work but, as in every experiment before it, compromises have to be made along the way. On the basis of what has already been done, the reader will decide if the founding ideals are likely to remain sufficiently in place to sustain a worthwhile experiment for the present century. More than that, will it succeed in influencing other comparable experiments and even to lead to a more generalised pattern of change?

Notes

1   Coates (2001), frontispiece
2   Ebenezer Howard, in Beevers (1988), p.184
3   Edward Akroyd, textile manufacturer, 1859, in Burnett (1978), p.177
4   Stewart (1952), p.154
5   Darley (1975)
6   Stewart (1952), p.173
7   Darley (1975), p.74
8   Marsh (1982), p.221
9   Bryson (1995), p.243
10 Darley (1975), p.96
11 Howard (1898), p.10
12 C.B. Purdom, in Hardy (2000), p.69
13 Armytage (1961), p.374
14 *Ibid.*
15 Marsh (1982), p.229
16 Miller (2002), p.76
17 *Ibid.*
18 *Ibid.*
19 *Daily Mail*, 27 March 1913
20 *The Race-Builder*, May 1906
21 Armytage (1961), p.381
22 Leslie Bilsby, in Michael Hebbert, 'The British Garden City: Metamorphosis', Chapter 9, in Ward (1992)
23 Michael Hebbert, *ibid.*
24 In 2004 the Town and Country Planning Association launched a project to apply garden city principles to the contemporary challenge of creating sustainable communities; while in the same year the Letchworth Garden City Heritage Foundation, in association with the University of Westminster, sponsored a fellowship to undertake a study to identify a meaningful future of the garden city idea
25 Samuel Taylor Coleridge, 1794, in making the case for his shared vision (with Robert Southey) of a prospective utopian society to be located in North America
26 The words accompanied a cartoon drawn by George Cruikshank, in *The Comic Almanack*, 1843
27 Ashbee, in Hardy (2000), p.114
28 *Ibid.*, p.116
29 *Ibid.*, p.118
30 Charles Rowley, in Hardy (2000), p.119
31 William Morris, in Hardy (2000), p.119
32 Eric Gill, in Hardy (2000), p.130
33 Dorothy Elmhirst, in Hardy (2000), p.147

Chapter 2

By Royal Design

*'We **can** build new developments which echo the familiar, attractive features of our regional vernacular styles. There **are** architects who can design with sensitivity and imagination so that people can live in more pleasant surroundings.'*[1]

Poundbury is the direct outcome of the Prince of Wales's belief that we can make a better job of our towns and cities. He has for many years been an outspoken critic of the failings of the architectural and planning professions and an advocate of a new set of guiding principles. As one of the country's major landowners he is also in the position to be able to put some of his, often controversial, ideas into practice. The new settlement of Poundbury is his most ambitious experiment to date.

A Princely Vision

'Everything cries out for a reappraisal of our values and attitudes. Don't be intimidated by those who deride such views. They have had their day.'[2]

The Prince has a vision but it is, to a large extent, the Duchy of Cornwall that exercises responsibility for turning it into practice. The Duchy is a powerful institution that has since the 14th century been organised to provide an income for the heir apparent; its 'main purpose is to cover the cost of the heir apparent's public and private life'.[3] The first beneficiary was Prince Edward (son of Edward III), best known as the Black Prince; the present Prince of Wales (Charles Philip Arthur George Mountbatten-Windsor), as the eldest surviving son of the monarch, continues this long tradition. Charles is, in fact, the twenty-fourth Duke of Cornwall.

The capital assets of the Duchy are not owned by the Prince but are held on his behalf.[4] Most of the assets are derived from extensive property holdings, which have been increased in recent years at the expense of other forms of capital and which have led to a significant increase in income (a rise of 20 per cent between 2003 and 2004). There are now extensive land and commercial property holdings in 25 counties, with a total area of more than 140,000 acres (the largest estates being in the south-west of England). The executive board for this extensive enterprise is chaired by the Prince in his role as Duke of Cornwall, and includes a number of traditional posts: the Lord Warden of the Stannaries, the Receiver General, the Attorney-General to the Prince of Wales, and the Secretary and Keeper of the Records. Behind this colourful but seemingly outmoded tapestry of historic roles is a thoroughly modern and successful approach to business. Added to this, the Treasury (as custodian of the public purse) also maintains a watchful eye over the financial security of the Duchy.

But there is another side to the Prince of Wales's activities, and while the two can in one sense go hand in hand it as well to note that there is also a well defined line between them. As well as his official role as Chairman of this significant commercial operation, the Prince is also, in personal terms, undoubtedly a visionary. He has held the title of Duke of Cornwall for more than half a century, since his mother, Elizabeth II, ascended to the throne in 1952, and he assumed management responsibility for the Duchy in 1969, at the age of 21. Throughout his adult life, with no early prospect of becoming King, he has espoused a wide variety of causes: his mission, he once explained, has been over the years 'entirely motivated by a desperate desire to put the *Great* back into Great Britain'.[5] Foremost amongst these causes is his desire for better planning and architecture, and related environmental issues of organic farming and sustainability. He has campaigned consistently on these issues and his integrity of belief can hardly be in doubt. The contradiction of his official position, however, is that there is inevitably a price tag attached to his visionary ideas. The Prince, for all his powers, cannot be a free agent and all

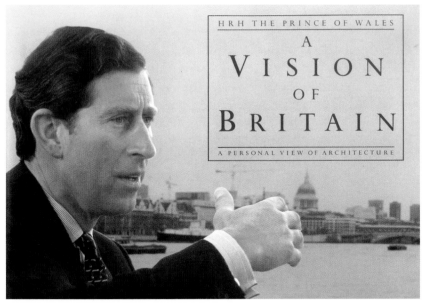

Cover illustration of A Vision of Britain, by the Prince of Wales

that he has done to promote his causes cannot be judged fairly without regard to this. Even if he were to want to indulge his plans to the exclusion of other activities, he would be prevented from doing so by his responsibilities to the Duchy. It is with this cautionary note that one can more objectively follow his path to a large parcel of his own land on the edge of the county town of Dorset, venue for his Poundbury experiment.

The first that most people heard about this project was in the course of a television programme originally broadcast in October 1988, and subsequently published as a book by the Prince of Wales, *A Vision of Britain*. The programme was devised and presented by the Prince himself to provide a platform to explain more fully than he had done before what he thought was wrong with modern architecture and town planning and to put forward some ideas for improvement. His basic message was simple and direct: that architects had too often turned their backs on the past and were persistently ignoring the needs of ordinary people. After his broadcast he demonstrated his populism by citing the evidence of correspondence, of which 99 per cent was in support of his ideas.

For some years previously the Prince had been attracting colourful media headlines with his unbridled criticism of modern architecture. He famously derided a proposed extension to the National Gallery as a 'monstrous carbuncle' and later condemned plans for a new convention centre in Birmingham (in words which he mischievously regarded as being as inoffensive as possible) as 'an unmitigated disaster'. Far from being isolated attacks, these objects of criticism were simply exemplars of a wider malaise: 'the wanton destruction which has taken place in this country in the name of progress; the sheer, unadulterated ugliness and mediocrity of public and commercial buildings, and of housing estates, not to mention the dreariness and heartlessness of so much urban planning'.[6]

Especially since the Second World War, successive waves of redevelopment failed miserably to create buildings and townscapes of character. Talk of creating a brave new world was hopelessly misguided in the face of the wholesale clearance of traditional neighbourhoods and their replacement by monotonous and often brutal environments. An irony was that comprehensive town planning legislation had been introduced after the war to shape the future of Britain's towns and countryside. Plans were quickly drawn up and a barrage of bureaucratic controls set in place, but the outcome was disappointing. The long arm of the State too often proved inadequate to the task of finding a home for life and humanity in new development.

It had been a bleak period but, so the Prince argued, there was no intrinsic reason why it should be allowed to continue. Architects had lost their way and planners were sometimes too immersed in bureaucratic tangles, yet there was indeed a means of escape. Most people could tell a good environment from a bad one and it was time to get back to basics; there is nothing wrong, the Prince asserted, with simplicity. So, as a guide for the future, he introduced ten principles that should be at the heart of a new approach.[7]

First there is *the place:* one must respect the land, and new buildings should be designed and sited so that they blend with the landscape. In order to protect the environment, new development should be compact.

Then there is *hierarchy:* the size of buildings should reflect their public importance, and the buildings themselves should be coherent. In a village, the church and pub are familiar landmarks but in modern developments there is often no obvious focus. Nor is there always a focus in the likes of new office blocks and hospitals, leaving the user lost and bemused.

A third principle is *scale:* buildings should be measured in terms of human proportions and should also take account of what is around them. There is no place in the Prince's architectural kit bag for high buildings that dwarf their surroundings, unless their very height, as in a cathedral, matches our lofty aspirations.

Harmony is another principle, where buildings are in tune with their neighbours. They can be of different styles but should always have regard to what is around them: 'singing with the choir and not against it'. Piecemeal redevelopment has often led to unnecessary disjunctures in the street scene.

Another principle is *enclosure:* market squares and walled gardens are widely valued but seldom provided in new developments. Wind-swept expanses between high buildings are no substitute for a genuine sense of enclosure where people can meet and feel secure.

The sixth principle is *materials*, where use is made of local geological characteristics to create distinctive regional townscapes. Modern technologies have produced a dull uniformity that extends not just across regional but also across national boundaries. A call is made to revive local features.

There should also be *decoration*, seen as a lost art in the face of standardised building techniques. A gap seems to have opened up between the modern architect, who has little time for decoration, and craftsmen who can handle stone and metalwork, rendering and decorative plasterwork.

It is a short step from decoration to *art:* the former being more concerned with repetition and pattern, the latter with something unique. Once art and architecture went hand in hand, with great works of art as an integral part of public and private buildings. But a gap has opened up between the two professions, a gap that needs to be closed in the search for common roots and synergies.

Signs and lights represent another area of concern, with a recognition that streets can be blighted by a profusion of regulatory signage, jarring adverts and inappropriate lighting. Proper attention to these commonplace features can help to transform the quality of streets and public places across the country.

Last but not least is *community*, which starts with the essential notion that people should have the opportunity to be involved in shaping their own environment. Planners are blamed for putting too much emphasis on zoning, with the separation of home and work leading to long journeys and fragmenting lifestyles. And invariably the car has been given pride of place, to the detriment of the quality of place. The Prince concludes that 'it is time for more experiment in the way we plan, build and own our communities'.

Having set out his stall, the way was open for schemes to lift the spirits and delight us by their scale and attention to every detail. Some examples of good new developments were cited and it was not unexpected that he has repeatedly proclaimed support for the works of neo-classical architects like Terry Farrell and Quinlan Terry, who were prepared to return to classical forms in the face of cries of 'pastiche' from modernists. Nor was it unexpected that the Prince looked back, not simply to earlier styles of building, but to traditional forms of settlement that seem to have worked.

But if the Prince looked back it was in order to look forward too, most notably in the form of his own ambitious plan. 'I'm hoping,' he concluded, 'to put some of these principles into practice in Dorchester.'[8] Poundbury, on the edge of Dorchester, was at that stage already more than a glimmer in the Prince's eye.

Designing the Future

'How do you get to this wondrous place – by railroad or rainbow?'[9]

Ideas are one thing, but the difficult task of turning them into reality is quite another. The number of utopian schemes that never left the drawing board far exceeds those that did, and even the latter characteristically fail to achieve even a small proportion of the original ideals. All manner of obstacles stand in the way of realisation: the scepticism and opposition of outsiders, the limitations of those who participate, a lack of resources and wherewithal to build the New Jerusalem, and very often too flaws in the scheme itself.

Poundbury, however, was never seen by the Prince as a utopian scheme. It was not intended to do the impossible, to rebuild all aspects of society; instead it focused very clearly on the physical fabric of the proposed settlement. Social changes might well follow but these were never a central part of the original vision. Thus, in taking it forward the Prince (under the watchful eye of the Duchy) was entirely practical, seeing it as his task to bring together the best talents available to build the new community. Probably the most inspired, and certainly crucial, stage in the whole experiment was to identify his key designers and to see where there were already exemplars of good development. In the event, Poundbury was to draw on four sources of inspiration.

One was to be found in the further development of the Prince's own ideas, advanced under the broad banner of 'traditional urbanism'; the second was through the movement known as New Urbanism, essentially American in origins but even at that time attracting international interest and application; the third was through the appointment of the Luxembourg architect and master-planner, Leon Krier, who although a founding father of New Urbanism would also bring to the table a distinctive European perspective; and the fourth stemmed from the fact that the site for the experiment was located not anywhere, but specifically in Dorset, and from a recognition that it would not succeed without use of the region's vernacular architecture (albeit with the addition of some universal classical features). These different sources were brought together in a remarkable way to shape the new settlement and to create something unique. In spite of different starting points, this alliance of ideas demonstrated a common commitment to traditional architectural form and values – and evidence of this is precisely what was to emerge in Poundbury.

The Prince and Traditional Urbanism

'The moment was right for a new campaign. There was a widespread enthusiasm for a more environmentally responsible approach to land use, transport and lifestyle...'[10]

In the above quote, David Lunts, a former Chief Executive of The Prince's Foundation for the Built Environment (explained below), looks back to the early 1990s and to the difficulties faced by advocates of what is variously termed 'traditional' or 'authentic' urbanism. He recalls that the publication of a report in 1992 on urban villages 'was greeted with rather more scepticism than enthusiasm'.[11] There was enough of the latter, though, to encourage a new campaign, and just ten years after that he was able to conclude that things looked very different. People were by then far more receptive to the whole notion of the new form of urban development that the Prince and others had been championing, and there were also welcome signs of government initiatives supporting this approach. Reference could also be made to the few schemes, including Poundbury, that demonstrated its advantages.

At the same time as making a start on Poundbury, the Prince also nurtured a parallel track of development of ideas as well as practical support for other schemes. The start of Poundbury itself stimulated a lively debate about urban form and, arising from that, 1998 saw the formation of The Prince's Foundation for the Built Environment. This proved to be an effective means not simply of advancing theory but also of encouraging good practice. The Foundation is described in its own publicity as 'a centre of excellence where these principles of urban design and architecture can be fostered and taught, not to replicate the past but so that today's buildings, towns and cities might benefit from that body of knowledge'.[12] It is often stressed that the whole movement is about far more than a simple reaction to modern architecture; the new approach has its own very distinctive coherence. It is also about making full use of modern technologies and meeting contemporary needs, as opposed simply to copying from the past.

While Poundbury is the Foundation's flagship it is by no means isolated, and quite a wide variety of schemes, in various stages of development, have been linked under the generic title of 'urban villages'. The very concept of an urban village is recognised by its own proponents as an oxymoron, 'but a concept that nevertheless conjures a vision of neighbourhood, of conviviality and character, within an urban environment on a far broader scale than the rural village'.[13] Launched as a campaign in 1990, the original Urban Villages Group (subsequently Forum) was later incorporated within The Prince's Foundation, as a means of promoting practical projects within cities as well as, like Poundbury, on greenfield sites.

The features that are sought in a planned urban village bear a remarkable affinity to the underlying principles of Poundbury, namely, to achieve a development of adequate size and critical mass; a walkable and pedestrian-friendly environment; a good mix of uses and good opportunities for employment; a varied architecture and a sustainable urban form; mixed tenure for both housing and employment uses; provision to meet basic shopping, health and educational needs; and a degree of self-sufficiency.[14]

Hank Dittmar is the present Chief Executive of The Prince's Foundation, having taken up office at the start of 2005.[15] He arrived with an unblemished pedigree in the United States as a leading exponent of New Urbanism, and is totally committed to a view of cities that are no longer built around the needs of the car and suburban mall developers. Settlements should be sufficiently compact and well designed to encourage people to walk for everyday needs and to use public transport for longer journeys. As Chairman of the Board of Directors for the Chicago-based Congress for the New Urbanism he is enthusiastic about the potential of what has become a trans-Atlantic movement. He sees working models as important to the Foundation's campaign and, while Poundbury more than adequately serves this purpose, he hopes that before long there will be others too. Preliminary work to extend the small coastal resort of Newquay, in Cornwall, suggests that this may soon help to fill this gap.

Trans-Atlantic Perspective: New Urbanism

'Our American colleagues talk about New Urbanism. Vice-President Al Gore spoke to me about liveability. I prefer to think of sustainable communities.'[16]

The term 'New Urbanism' was derived in the United States, referring to a movement that emerged largely in response to the excruciating failure of urban planning to curb the excesses of seemingly endless suburban sprawl coupled with the demise of town centres.[17]

In the suburbs it was not the planners but the real estate lobby, car manufacturers, gasoline distributors and the retail mall operators who were primarily responsible for an amorphous landscape devoid of civic and environmental values. At the same time, many of the traditional downtown areas had become 'no go' areas, a product of low property values and a high incidence of crime amongst those who remained. It was (and still is) a sorry picture, but at least sufficient to evoke an overdue response from elements of the design professions. Two architect planners, Andres Duany and Elizabeth Plater-Zyberk, were amongst a small but influential group of American architects who assumed a leading role in questioning the inevitability of what had gone before and helping to shape an alternative approach. Significantly, in terms of Poundbury's history, Leon Krier was also heavily involved in this type of critique from the outset.

Architects have always favoured the announcement of new directions through manifestoes, most notably as happened nearly a century ago through the inauguration of an international movement to promote modernism. In this same tradition, in 1993 there was already sufficiently wide support and understanding of this new approach for a Congress to be convened and subsequently for the publication of a Charter of essential principles (the Charter of the New Urbanism).[18] The wording of the Charter is geared closely to the American situation but the basic message is absolutely fundamental to an understanding of Poundbury.

In certain respects, New Urbanism is not really new at all, and the alternative term 'neo-traditionalism' perhaps better defines what it is trying to achieve. A helpful definition is provided by the British researcher Stephen Marshall, who sees it as 'effectively an urban design package that combines neo-traditional style buildings arranged in street grids to form relatively dense, walkable mixed-use neighbourhoods'.[19] In other words, the aim might be to re-create the conditions that were typical of a traditional English market town, an historic European centre or a New England colonial settlement.

The very prospect of re-creating anything traditional is a bone of contention for modernist architects, and New Urbanists have had constantly to rebut this source of criticism. Demetri Porphyrios, in arguing the case for Leon Krier's work, denies that there is anything 'in the traditional city that makes it incompatible with contemporary technology, economy and lifestyle'. In spite of the lambasting by 'experts' he maintains that traditionalism is generally very popular with ordinary people, concluding that 'perhaps, after all, the lay public may not be so kitsch and dumb as it is portrayed by the *avant-gardists* of neo-modernism'. He goes on to praise the work of Krier as 'the celebration of traditional urban life itself'.[20]

In spite of its traditional leanings, at the end of the 20th century New Urbanism marked a radical change of direction. In particular, in the British context, it represented a challenge to a form of planning that, in spite of rhetoric to the contrary, still weighted decisions in favour of the car; showed reluctance to shed an historic preference for land use zoning that dates from an industrial era when housing was cheek by jowl with smoky factories; had effectively disembowelled town centres with several decades of encouragement for out-of-town shopping; had come nowhere near to addressing problems of social exclusion; and had failed miserably to foster standards of architecture that people would actually like. Beyond an essential need to correct past failings there was also a new environmental agenda, focused around the issue of sustainability. Buildings have to be more environmentally friendly but so, too, does the very layout of new development, with a reduction of car journeys being just one important objective.

In the various sections of the Charter of New Urbanism is a clear indication of what needs to be done and, no less, a very clear explanation of why Poundbury is emerging as it is. If the guidelines are followed, New Urbanist settlements should be identifiable, with a sharp urban edge and coherent neighbourhoods and districts. The neighbourhoods should be compact, socially and functionally mixed, and pedestrian friendly; there is an emphasis on using design to encourage a sense of community and shared responsibility for the area. Shops, schools and public buildings should be embedded in neighbourhoods, not isolated in single-use zones; with, ideally, everyday facilities within a short walk from the home. Those who do not drive – especially the young and old – should not be disadvantaged from enjoying access to a full range of social facilities. A range of parks 'from tot-lots and village greens to ballfields and community gardens' should be distributed through the neighbourhoods, with open farmland and other large expanses of open land defining the urban edge.

Buildings should be designed in a series of linked 'urban blocks' in which streets and public spaces are recovered as places of common use and civic pride. Cars should be accommodated but not to the exclusion of safe use of spaces by the pedestrian. Importance is attached to symbolic architecture and attractions such as fountains in civic places, restoring something of the urban splendour that was typical of historic centres with their cathedrals and *maisons de ville*. No less important, architecture should be shaped by its surroundings and by local building traditions.

New Urbanism can offer a number of working models to illustrate these principles and priorities, one of which is Seaside, Florida, conceived in a traditional style of pastel-coloured clapboard houses with porches and balconies. Seen as something of a showcase for New Urbanism, and historically a decade or so ahead of Poundbury, it is understandable that many involved with the English experiment have made the trans-Atlantic journey to see what has been done; in this vein, we return to Seaside in a later chapter. More immediately, the New Urbanist guru Andres Duany has worked closely on schemes with Leon Krier and was for a short time directly involved in an aspect of the early planning of Poundbury.

Leon Krier: Modernity not Modernism

'Ten years ago when you talked about streets and squares you were considered a bit of a nostalgic, or out of touch with your time. This is no longer so.' [21]

Second only to the Prince of Wales, Leon Krier is a key figure in the emergence of Poundbury. Beyond professional circles, he would have been largely unknown to the British public at the time of his appointment as the new town's master-planner. The observant reader would have spotted an interesting line sketch in the Prince's book, illustrating the kind of settlement Poundbury could be, and an adulatory note alongside declaring that 'Leon Krier is brilliant at setting down a vision for a town or city'.[22] Soon, though, with the production of his plans the missing details of his background and reputation

Leon Krier in his home village in the South of France

were filled in. Born in Luxembourg, he had lived in London for 20 years before making his home in the South of France. The author of an important book, *Architecture: Choice or Fate*, he is typically described as 'the intellectual godfather of the New Urbanism movement in America'.[23] Appropriately, before embarking on the Poundbury scheme, he had contributed to the design of Seaside.

Leon Krier is the quintessential European: multi-lingual, highly cultured, a brilliant musician, an architect who sets his skills in a philosophical context. He enjoys the confidence of the Prince and exercises an enormous influence on the development of Poundbury; as the master-planner he has played a major part not only in shaping the new town but also in determining its architectural character. His models of inspiration are to be found in the great European cities, in Italian hill towns and in villages hewn from local stone; cathedrals and towers, fountains and monuments, bustling streets, pedestrian links and formal squares are his building blocks. Given the importance that he attaches to the space between buildings and the link between detailed design and civic experience, it is little wonder he has been likened to the classic urban designer, Camillo Sitte.

Recalling the destruction by post-1945 planners and architects of the hitherto enduring traditions of his beloved homeland, Krier has been a consistent and outspoken critic of modernism. Faced with a choice, he asks, would anyone really miss anything that has been built across the world since 1945 compared with all that was built before? The recent legacy of modernism has been dominant over the past half century and yet is widely reviled; in contrast, the pre-1945 legacy is just as widely cherished. Responding to these differences, Krier argues that there are other ways of embracing modernity than simply following the pattern of recent development. One can look back to past traditions while at the same time embracing modern technologies and meeting modern needs: there are already examples in various countries of a form of modernity 'that is not alienating, kitsch or aggressive but serene and urbane'.[24]

Atlantis: Designed by Leon Krier, 1987. Watercolour by Rita Woolf (Courtesy: Leon Krier)

Krier's notion of modernity is everything that modernism is not. Whereas the latter is collectivist and alienating, the former is essentially democratic; while modernism builds in concrete, glass and steel, a more traditional approach will use materials gathered locally; the one fragments the city into functional zones, the other seeks to bring the various parts together; modernism builds high, traditionalism uses height only for buildings of civic importance or as landmarks. Urban life should be on a human scale and, for Krier, the urban block is the key to good urban design: these blocks should be 'as small in length as typologically viable; they should form as many well-defined streets and squares as possible in the form of a *multi-directional horizontal pattern of urban spaces'*.[25]

Before taking on the task of planning Poundbury, Krier had produced a series of extraordinary designs (not all of which were subsequently built) for a variety of clients. His most ambitious scheme was his master-plan for Atlantis, a proposed new town on the Atlantic island of Tenerife, designed in an uncompromising classical mould. Although the plan has remained on the drawing board it provided a colourful portent of things to come. The main features were straight from ancient Greece and Rome, including an acropolis and agora and an array of public buildings complete with columns and arches, pyramids and obelisks, pediments and vaults. Stone was the dominant building material, together with wood and tile. Elsewhere, Krier has made his mark with designs for villas and village restorations plans, for public spaces and monuments. All are unmistakeably traditional in one form or another and his selection by the Prince to design Poundbury must have been an easy one to make, and one which suited both parties. Here at last, for Krier, was a conceptual challenge that, unlike Atlantis, stood a very real chance of realisation. The stage was set for a fascinating meeting of cultures and ideas that were to be at the very heart of the new Dorset settlement.

Vernacular Meets Classical

'Traditional architecture comprises two complementary faces: vernacular building, on the one hand, classical or monumental architecture on the other.' [26]

Vernacular and classical are not at first sight obvious bed-mates; the first is associated more with the local and geared to everyday life, the latter more to do with the grand and for special occasions. Dictionary definitions of vernacular as being domestic and indigenous, and classical as being of the highest class, bear out this distinction. For advocates of traditional architecture, such as Leon Krier, the challenge is to achieve the potential richness of the two by bringing both together, not as an incoherent hybrid but as compatible partners. Each speaks in its own way of a particular lineage.

Vernacular building is 'the artisan culture of construction',[27] and will most commonly be seen in the style of houses and other buildings in everyday use. These are the products of the local craftsman using materials that are easily to hand and designed to meet particular climatic and other demands. Unlike the classical, and certainly unlike modernism, it is this responsiveness to local geological and other conditions that leads to colourful variety from one area to another. Traditionalists are keen to recognise these differences and to carry forward unique patterns that have been developed over centuries. Although the site of Poundbury was practically devoid of buildings at the start of the project its wider setting is one that Krier and others were keen to acknowledge.

Thomas Hardy's cottage, Higher Bockhampton, Dorset

Dorset vernacular architecture is characterised by enormous variety, itself a reflection of the complexity of the county's geology, such that the bedrock of one valley can be contrasted with that of the next. Buildings are typified by the copious use of local stone, which in itself exhibits great variations in colour, texture and resilience. The county's cottages, often thatched, are the very epitome of a rural idyll and perhaps nowhere better fits this stereotype than the cottage at Higher Bockhampton, just four miles from Poundbury, where the Dorset writer Thomas Hardy was born and lived for the early part of his life. This is where Hardy grew up and wrote two of his famous novels, *Under the Greenwood Tree* and *Far from the Madding Crowd*. Hardy's Cottage (now carefully maintained by the National Trust) is everything that one thinks of as a country cottage. It is made of two-foot thick walls of cob, the ultimate vernacular building material (composed of gravel, chalk, clay and flint, with straw as binding and water to mix it all together). Brick has been added to face the cob; local timber is used for the beams and wheat thatch on the roof. In the garden are enduring country favourites: monkshood and lupins, Solomon's seal and cornflower, rosemary and lavender.

As an advocate of the vernacular, David Oliver was the West Dorset District Council's Chief Architect before he was commissioned by the Duchy to advise

Abbotsbury: a pioneering scheme in the locality that pre-dates Poundbury

on Poundbury's detailed design and development.[28] In his previous employment he pioneered, with fellow officers and the support of councillors, a new respect for the vernacular, largely in response to public opposition to characterless new development around the county. He tells of the impact of a particular case close to Bridport, a small town some 15 miles to the west of Poundbury, where a totally inappropriate village extension led to a public outcry and calls for a more sensitive approach in future. The then chair of the Planning Committee, John Lock, saw in this a mandate to commission a new approach, and David Oliver was charged with taking it forward. Responding enthusiastically to the brief, Oliver saw it partly as a question of design advice but also as a need for more flexibility on highways issues. He was able to put his ideas to the test in two subsequent schemes in outlying villages, where in both cases the outcome was that new development gave the appearance of being there as long as surrounding older buildings; use of local stone, thatched roofs and careful detailing were key components.[29] The public response was very favourable and the reputation of the local planning authority was enhanced in the process. A firm local foundation had thus been laid a few years before Poundbury itself made the headlines.

In contrast with the vernacular, classical architecture looks more towards high art and monumental design. Whereas the vernacular is largely functional, the classical embraces the symbolic; it is concerned, says Krier, 'with the construction and decoration of public structures, with buildings, squares, and monumental features in general'.[30] It can be adapted to local conditions – as in some of the grander private houses – but essentially it retains the features of its classical origins in Greece and Rome, which are then universally applied. It was planned from the outset that in Poundbury there would be a mix of the truly vernacular and the 'high art' of classical features. Templates for the latter would be borrowed from existing fine buildings in the locality, such as the Palladian style of country houses, Georgian buildings originally designed for wealthy tradesmen in the centre of Dorchester, and imposing merchants' houses overlooking Weymouth harbour. Traditionally these have sat well alongside simpler and more modest structures and there was no reason why they could not do so again in a different setting.

Notes

1   Prince of Wales (1989), p.15
2   *Ibid.*, p.156
3   http://www.princeofwales.gov.uk
4   HRH The Prince of Wales, Annual Review 2004, Clarence House. See http://www.princeofwales.gov.uk/about/annual review_2004
5   'The Prince's Role', http://www.prince of wales.gov.uk
6   Prince of Wales (1989), p.7
7   *Ibid.*, pp.75-97
8   *Ibid.*, p.138
9   Sceptical question of a visitor to a 19th-century American community, in Hardy (1979), Preface
10 David Lunts, in Neal, ed. (2003), Afterword
11 The report referred to by Lunts was the product of the Urban Villages Group, led by Trevor Osborne
12 http://www.princes-foundation.org
13 Prince of Wales, in Neal, ed. (2003), Preface
14 Neal, ed. (2003), p.11
15 Interview with Hank Dittmar, Chief Executive and Ben Bolgar, Director of Design, The Prince's Foundation, 14 February 2005
16 Deputy Prime Minister, John Prescott, speaking on a visit to The Prince's Foundation, 20 November 2003. See http://www.odpm.gov.uk
17 See, for instance, an interesting collection of articles in a special edition of *Built Environment*, Vol. 29, No. 3, 2003
18 There are various entries to the Congress of the New Urbanism (CNU) on the Web. For instance, see Charter of the New Urbanism, http://www.newurbanism.org/pages/532096. For a fuller account with commentaries, see Leccese, M. and McCormick, K., eds. (2000)
19 Stephen Marshall, 'New Urbanism: An Introduction', *Built Environment*, Vol. 29, No. 3, p.189
20 Demetri Porphyrios, in Economakis, ed. (1992), p.10

21 Krier, 1981, in 'Leon Krier' by David Watkins, in Economakis, ed. (1992), p.13
22 Prince of Wales (1989), p.139
23 J.H. Kunstler, in N. Salingaros, 'The future of cities: the absurdity of modernism', http://www.planetizen.com/oped/item.php?id=35
24 Krier (1998), p.16
25 Krier, in Miller, M., 'Poundbury, Dorchester: British New Urbanism or picturesque illusion?' Paper presented at the Tenth Biennial Conference on Planning History of the Society for American City and Regional Planning History, St Louis, Missouri, 6-9 November 2003
26 Krier (1998), p.53
27 Ibid.
28 Interview with David Oliver, 21 January 2005
29 The two schemes were at Broad Windsor and Abbotsbury
30 Ibid.

Chapter 3

Making Plans

'We will try to make some small piece of English ground, beautiful, peaceful and fruitful'[1]

J ohn Ruskin's quest in the 19th century to make some small piece of English ground beautiful, peaceful and fruitful has a resonance in this contemporary attempt at Poundbury to find new ways to recover lost values. Ruskin, however, could see little good in his modern world and was unwilling to embrace the potential benefits of new technologies. Poundbury, in contrast, seeks to bring forward what is good from the past but within a wholly modern context. Striking a balance between old and new is a tricky manoeuvre and a constant source of comment for critics.

From the outset, the plans for Poundbury have encouraged more questions than answers. What is it really about? Is it an attempt to recapture a lost past or a model for the future? Is it a middle-class idyll or a place for everyone? Is it merely the indulgence of a rich Prince or a ground-breaking vision? Such questions are hardly surprising given the heady mix of characters and circumstances involved: the conservative setting of a small county town, the personal involvement of the Prince himself, the leading role of a continental architect, and even the ghost of Thomas Hardy with a reminder not just of the beautiful Dorset countryside but also of the hovering presence of potential tragedy. The planning of Poundbury – no matter how well founded – was never going to be without contention.

A Time and Place

'Obviously the participation of the people of Dorchester is needed, and hard economic calculations have to be made, before any building can start, but vision and boldness are also needed if we are to produce something of real beauty in the English countryside.'[2]

When the wronged wife in Thomas Hardy's *The Mayor of Casterbridge* first set sight on the town that was, in reality, Dorchester, she found it 'huddled all together, and shut in by a square wall of trees'. It was the squareness of the place that most caught her attention, and with what (in the light of current developments) proved to be extraordinary irony, she observed that 'it was untouched by the faintest sprinkle of modernism'.[3]

A statue of Thomas Hardy stands at the top of the High Street, keeping a watchful eye over Dorchester's continuing history. For most of the past century the compactness and squareness of the town that Hardy described in his Victorian novel has remained intact to a remarkable degree. There are a few points where it has broken through its Victorian boundaries, but change has come slowly. As a small county town with a thriving market and many fine buildings, aspects of Dorchester even to the present day would be comfortably familiar to Hardy and his contemporaries.

Dorchester is one of those settlements that can be read as a palimpsest of England's long and often chequered history. Nearby Maiden Castle was first settled in pre-Roman times, the site of an important Iron Age hill fort, although in the year 43 AD unable to resist the might of the invading Roman army. Shortly after the invasion, a settlement, Durnovaria, was established by the occupying force on

Thomas Hardy: keeping watch on modern Dorchester

the site of later Dorchester, and its layout was the cause of what Hardy in his time observed as the 'squareness' of the town. Durnovaria became Dornwecestre in Saxon times and Dorecestre at the time of Domesday, its main function in its mediaeval days being its market. Successive periods were to leave their mark on the architecture of the town, especially the Georgian and Victorian, but in spite of Hardy's gloomy observation in 1910 that 'like all other provincial towns [Dorchester] will lose its individuality – has lost much of it already',[4] the county town has survived change better than most.

Not until the 1980s was there a serious threat to Dorchester's historic form. At the start of that decade the local authorities (Dorset County Council and West Dorset District Council) anticipated a need to release land for new development for employment as well as housing. A document was published by the District Council, setting out options for expansion and pointing in particular to an area on the eastern edge of the town, close to the River Frome and its much valued water meadows. With the building of a ring road in that same decade, in a wide sweep around much of the outer boundary of the town, coupled with the Prince's interest in his own scheme, attention was then re-focused to the western periphery. The ring road had overnight created an extensive reservoir of potential development land, more suitable in many ways than earlier options. With pressures for development increasing, had this opportunity been anywhere else the outcome would have been predictable: a

Attractive features of Dorchester town centre

consortium of housing developers sub-dividing the land into discrete estates with token supporting facilities, coupled, no doubt, with an out-of-town retail park. The bland character of some previous, relatively small-scale, development on the edge of Dorchester hardly indicated that it would have been any better. But in this case the essential difference was that the most suitable parcel of potential building land – some 400 acres – was owned (through the Duchy of Cornwall) by the Prince of Wales. Through a happy coincidence of time and place an approach in 1987 by the local authority to the Duchy was well received.

Centred on Poundbury and Middle Farms, the Duchy had owned land in the district since the 14th century, and this particular stretch of countryside had been farmed throughout its settled history. Even before this, the Romans had given it a wide berth for their settlement, preferring the more sheltered site that was to become Dorchester to the wind-swept ridge of Poundbury to the west. Given the Prince's declared views and its development potential, the availability of this land proved to be just the opportunity for an experimental scheme of his own making. The ideas were there, and so was the land; now was the time for action.

Discussions between West Dorset District Council and the Duchy were already well advanced before the publication of the Prince's book in 1989, and while there was initial agreement on the principle of town expansion, both parties came to the table with their own starting positions. The demands of the District Council were straightforward: new housing was the priority and some of it would have to be accessible to lower-income groups. In turn, the Duchy, echoing the Prince's own priorities, asserted that new development should form an urban rather than suburban extension to Dorchester, a place where people could work as well as live. There should be in its architecture a healthy respect for 'the traditions of the past while looking forward to the requirements of the 21st century'.[5] It is said that what the Prince had in mind was to be able to stand one day on the fortifications along the ridge of Maiden Castle and not be confronted by a blot on the remarkable Dorset landscape. How, though, to achieve such an aspiration? What could be done at Poundbury that had not already been done elsewhere?

The clarity of the Prince's vision was an important start but beyond that lay a potential minefield of public consultation and planning committees. In fact, there was an easier option: Poundbury could have been developed without recourse to the authorities, under ancient rights of Crown exemption, but the Prince chose wisely to take the more tortuous route. One reason was that he wanted to do something that could be replicated elsewhere without special privileges; another reason was that to invoke Crown exemption would undoubtedly have attracted additional criticism, on the grounds of spurning democratic processes. The result was that the way ahead was far from easy. For a start, in seeking to break the mould the Prince's architectural preferences were not always to win easy favour with officials and their panoply of regulations. Not that this type of confrontation was new: nearly a century earlier, the progressive architects Raymond Unwin and Barry Parker had to get a change to building bye-laws in order to include the innovative *cul-de-sac* in their enlightened scheme at Hampstead Garden Suburb. In the case of Poundbury there were a number of similar touchstones.

Planners, for instance, are notoriously cautious about the idea of mixing land uses (a legacy of justifiable attempts to separate housing from the smoke and noise of 19th-century factories and mines). It took a while to convince them of the merits of dispersing light industry and offices around the settlement rather than concentrating it all in one or two zones. Not only does a mix of uses lead to better management of traffic, but it also avoids the disadvantages of parts of a town being deserted out of working hours. There was also (rather like the historic precedent of the *cul-de-sac*) lengthy discussion about the acceptability of courtyards within the housing areas, a feature that the local authority declared its unwillingness to adopt as a future council responsibility. And highway engineers, wedded to their own models of turning circles and parking allocations, proved in the early stages particularly difficult to persuade.

Some ten years after the protracted negotiations, the Prince spoke to an audience of MPs of the then House of Commons Committee on the Environment, Transport and the Regions. He echoed the views of many a developer in accusing 'professional bodies, including road traffic engineers and the building research establishment' of clinging stubbornly to a '1960s mindset' that left them unable to think beyond building soulless housing estates. While he conceded that attitudes were changing, he singled out planners for being slow to relax long-held views on zoning and to allow a greater mix of housing, shops, business units and leisure activities.

The Prince also accepts that he erred in his early choice of master-planners who themselves favoured a zoned approach which was altogether too conventional to meet the challenge of creating something really new.[6] The last thing wanted was just another suburban housing estate. The Prince responded quickly in passing the brief to Leon Krier, urging him to be radical.

Within a year, in 1989, Krier had produced his first version of Poundbury's master-plan and presented it to a five-day *charette* (a word meaning workshop, much loved in New Urbanist circles for its function of bringing together the various professions and stakeholders to agree common principles)[7] located in a marquee at Poundbury Farm. In spite of Duchy concerns that what was proposed would prove to be expensive, and a feeling that it needed to pay more respect to local styles, the plan enjoyed the support of the Prince and in due course won wider agreement. In any case, Krier took the view that 'if they, the community, didn't like what he was up to he'd go home and they could have the usual stuff'.[8]

Nor was the Prince beyond the reach of economic constraints in the housing market. He was always eager to press ahead, but his advisers in the Duchy offices would undoubtedly have counselled restraint in the face of a collapsing housing market at the end of the 1980s. For this reason as much as any it was not until 1993 that builders went onto the site, and it was a year later before the first houses were completed. There was also the question of winning local support. The Prince might well be a populist but it was by no means a foregone conclusion that he would convince a basically conservative populace of the merits of his plans to expand their town by a third (from Dorchester's population of about 15,000 to a planned total of at least 20,000).

In fact, it was not so much the idea of development that aroused the greatest concerns (most people were already resigned to its inevitability in one form or another) as the prospect of a novel style of architecture. The Prince had asked Leon Krier to produce something out of the ordinary and the resultant plan was to attract a response in kind.

Poundbury on the Drawing Board

'The most beautiful cities which survive in the world today have all been conceived with buildings of between two and five floors ... the day of the utilitarian skyscraper is at an end.'[9]

It is hard to imagine a more conservative setting for a radical experiment. Although Dorchester is only a few miles from Tolpuddle, the trade unionists' radical shrine in celebration of the 'martyrs' who suffered transportation in the 19th century, the town itself is steeped in its own, more conventional, traditions. Even accounting for the measured ways of an historic county town,

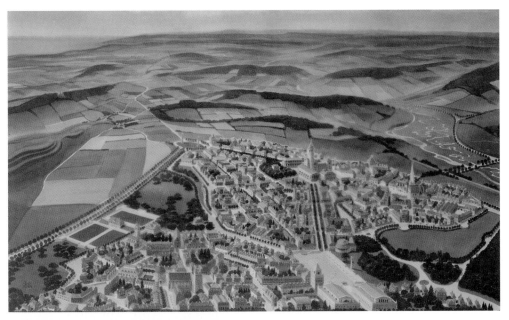

Above: Watercolour by Ed Venn, based on a drawing by Leon Krier, showing how Poundbury might look

Left: Painting by Carl Laubin, 1992, based on a drawing by Leon Krier, visualising a market hall and tower in the first town square

Britain as a nation has always been wary of importing architectural ideas (witness the opposition to modernist architects from continental Europe in the 1930s and 1940s). The very demeanour of Krier, a continental intellectual personified, was admirable in itself but destined to feed preconceptions of cultural difference to those who wanted to read things that way. When he first presented his master-plan, coupled with an indication of building style, there was talk amongst councillors that Poundbury was being planned in the image of an Italian hill town, unsuited to its Dorset surroundings. Add to this the context of an architectural profession looking for an opportunity to get its own back for the Prince's constant vilification of modern works and the scene was set for a lively exchange of views, nationally as well as locally.

Leading architects like Max Hutchinson, then the RIBA President, and architectural critic Martin Pawley opened the debate with a mixture of scorn and ridicule. Poundbury, they claimed, was a totally misguided concept that would never materialise, and, if even some of it did, it would represent a long outmoded style of architecture. Krier himself responded quickly to early criticisms, from local as well as national quarters, by modifying his plans to embrace more closely the characteristics of building in the Dorset vernacular, making good use of local materials, and with the promise of commissioning local architects familiar with these conditions. This commitment, far from offering reassurance, merely served to trigger a second wave of diatribe, ridiculing the plans as a 'blueprint for Toytown', 'an opera set from Bohemia' and 'a Thomas Hardy timewarp'. What irked external critics most was that this image of Poundbury seemed to ignore the present in favour of an imagined past, and most certainly made no concessions to accommodate the best of modern architecture. But this was a metropolitan view, a discernible sneer from the café bars and designer restaurants of London, and not, as the situation evolved, to be shared in the panelled meeting rooms of Dorchester.

In contrast, once they had recovered from the initial shock of encountering something so different from the normal pattern of new development, local reactions became generally supportive. Public meetings and workshops were arranged and events organised to encourage discussion groups; on occasion the Prince himself would join these meetings, arriving unannounced in his helicopter, to hear what people were saying and to offer his own thoughts. Following a presentation in 1991 to show detailed drawings for the first phase of development, local councillors gave their blessing to the scheme. They acknowledged that important changes had been made to ensure that the plans were more closely matched to Dorset conditions than the original ideas: it is no longer 'Florence-on-Frome' (referring to the river that runs through Dorchester) remarked one councillor. There was also a welcome to the inclusion of low-cost homes (amounting to 20 per cent of the first 244 houses). Dorchester Civic Society, a potential source of opposition to greenfield development, also threw its own weight behind the scheme, taking issue with some of the details but supporting the project as a whole.

A novel architectural style is always likely to grab the headlines, although for councillors and planning officers there were other features that seemed to represent a greater challenge to convention. Since the very inception of the modern planning system it had been a golden rule that industry and housing should be kept apart, but now there were plans to mix them. Another golden rule was to ensure that new housing contained enough off-street parking and driveways to get cars off the road, yet here was this New Urbanist philosophy which actually encouraged more on-street parking to slow down traffic. At the same time, in a dramatic reversal of planning priorities, Poundbury was designed 'starting with a sense of place rather than the vehicle'.[10] Finally, a long tradition of advocating lower housing densities (a conventional suburban norm has been 10 to 12 houses per acre) was being overturned in favour of development more in the range of 15 to 20 per acre. Ironically, these were all conditions that were commonplace in traditional towns like Dorchester itself but the idea of planning for them in a new settlement was one on which the authorities took more than a little convincing.

While building proceeded in the first phase (started in 1993), plans were prepared for the rest of the development. An outline application was submitted to the planning authority in 1996, based on Krier's master-plan, to be followed

The Prince of Wales at the first site meeting, in 1993 (Courtesy: Duchy of Cornwall)

stage by stage over a 10- to 15-year period with detailed plans. Ironically, the master-plan itself was not submitted for formal approval in the first two phases; it had always been anticipated that its later adoption by the local authority would serve to guide the remaining development. In fact, new planning legislation in 2004 confused the issue, as the final say on further development was moved from the county and district councils to a non-elected regional assembly for the whole of the South West. Theoretically, it is possible that further development could be stalled in favour of growth elsewhere in the region, although politically such a *volte-face* seems unlikely.

Apart from this potential planning hiatus, the continued growth of Poundbury will, in any case, become increasingly subject to challenge. Once the original principles of development had been accepted for Phase 1, the approval of detailed plans for the different sections within it was relatively uncontentious. In contrast, for later phases, with a larger population in place, new schemes will attract greater scrutiny and likely objections; everyone will want to have their say on what follows. Even in an innovative place like Poundbury, it is not long before 'nimbyism' makes its mark. Proposals which have already met with resistance include the parkway, which is intended to take through-traffic out of central Poundbury; a high-density scheme for

The Prince of Wales, with Leon Krier, Andrew Hamilton (Development Director, on the left) and Simon Conibear (Development Manager, on the right), in the leading group on one of the regular site visits (Courtesy: Duchy of Cornwall)

apartments which was turned back on account of the intensity of development; and an unsuccessful attempt to increase the proportion of social housing to 50 per cent in one section.

From Codes to Construction

'Many sound urban plans have been compromised by inflexible zoning codes and standards. A new set of design codes should replace the existing ones.'[11]

It is one thing to look for historical precedent and to spell out various principles in the heady atmosphere of an international gathering of architects and planners, and quite another to find the means to translate all of this into a consistent pattern of local schemes. The means that New Urbanists favour is that of design codes. There should, first, be a master-plan or framework to provide a grand vision, and then codes to give detailed guidance to those who will turn the big ideas into practice. The urban designer Paul Murrain describes a code as a mediating document, 'a set of instructions for how town, village, or neighbourhood should be designed and built'.[12] There is nothing new about the use of codes, he argues, as historically there have always had to be rules to give certainty to investors while at the same time reflecting collective values. They are, he concludes, 'the rules for the public realm, set out in a clear and ordered fashion, in advance of any private/individual input'.[13]

Leon Krier, himself, explains how a sensible application of codes can be achieved through a hierarchy of planning and implementation.[14] A master-plan, he argues, falls into four parts. The first is the master-plan itself, which maps out the general profile of the new development, indicates the distribution of street blocks and squares, and defines plot sizes. The second part is what he calls the urban code, which stipulates the allowed position of buildings on plots, the proportion to be occupied by development, and building heights. Next, there is the architectural code, describing the likes of materials and building characteristics; whether or not, for instance, to include chimney pots as a roofscape feature. If properly executed, the architectural code should allow responsibility to be passed to builders, with the architect in an advisory role. Finally, there is a series of codes for the public spaces and features such as arcades, fountains, spires and gates. Krier's hierarchy is, in short, a means to provide effective links between the client, master-planner,

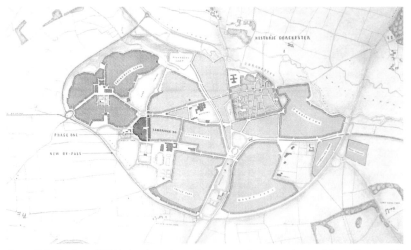

Leon Krier's plan, 1989, to show how the new urban quarters of Poundbury will form a natural extension to those of Dorchester

architects and builders and, through the use of interlocking codes, represents a procedure that has been followed, to different degrees, in Poundbury. The strength of codes lies in their ability to improve communication between the various parties involved in the building process and achieve the consistency and adherence to basic principles contained in the master-plan.

To take, first, the generalised master-plan, Krier was at pains to promote Poundbury as a new district for Dorchester, not turning its back on the old town but evolving organically from what is already there; it is planned, quite simply, as a town extension. Then, within Poundbury, he arranged its development in four discrete urban quarters, with no one quarter to have more than 800 households and some less (to accommodate a total population of at least 5000). The size of each of the urban quarters is determined by the time it would take to walk from one side to the other, no more than ten minutes; this would allow everyone to be within walking distance of a shared town centre. Buildings and spaces were arranged first, with the roads fitted around these (the reverse of more conventional plans, where the road network determines everything else). It would be a high-density development, more like old Dorchester than a traditional suburban extension, and much of the housing was planned around mews development, lanes, squares and courtyards.

Andres Duany was called in to assist in preparing a code for the next stage of development, to bridge the gap between the master-plan and detailed

*Leon Krier's master-plan for
Phase 1*

guidance for builders. In association with Krier and others he produced the
Poundbury Code, which he termed a Regulating Plan and which was intended
to assume legal standing that would supersede other regulations in force. It was
to be enforced through a specially designated Poundbury Code Committee. In
practice, it proved to be too bureaucratic and not as necessary as in the
American context, where the process was conceived in the first place and where
planning regulations are less finely grained. The alternative was to make the
jump through a manual (re-named the Poundbury Building Code) for local
architects and builders, to assist them in translating general principles into
practice; this is in addition to the normal planning, building and highway
regulations.[15] This is 'essentially a contract between a developer/builder and the
municipality... It gives the builder/developer certain rights and requires in
return the fulfilment of certain standards.'[16]

The Building Code provides detailed guidance on the likes of appropriate building materials, roof angles and window detail; and on common features such as external walls and the inclusion of traditional chimneys on each roof (even though very few are used for coal or wood fires). To illustrate the level of detail specified, the requirement for external walls is that materials should be restricted to one of three types.

First, use may be made of stone, but only from one of five named quarries in the locality; it will normally be split rather than sawn and will generally be random in size. Secondly, if bricks are used the type and colour has first to be agreed by the Duchy, and it is expected that these will normally be hand-made or stock bricks. A third option is to use rendered concrete blocks but to ensure that finishing is roughcast or wood-floated to avoid too exact a finish. There is also guidance on how a combination of these basic materials can be achieved to good effect. Additionally, details are provided on permitted mortar mixes and renderings, and on the painting of brick walls with a lime-tallow wash. Outbuildings will usually be timber framed and clad with weather-boarding, but ingenuity is encouraged to produce 'a charming variety of materials'.[17]

Attention is also paid to the kind of detail that so often mars the appearance of houses, and builders are required to ensure that various items will not be visible from the street: such as clothes driers, meter boxes, air extractors, wall ventilation openings and dustbins. Provision must also be made for cabled terrestrial as well as satellite television to avoid unsightly equipment on roofs and walls. In defence of traditional materials, there is a veto on the use of frosted glass (even for bathrooms).

The general aim is to encourage a good variety of materials and styles but within the bounds of a common design philosophy. It is accepted that the requirement for high-quality building materials has a cost (generally, such materials are 10-15% more expensive than those used in standard housing), but this can be passed on to house-buyers willing to pay for something that is more than a run-of-the-mill outcome. The Code is designed to uphold standards, but there is a fine balance to be struck between achieving consistency and still allowing room for innovation. For this reason some exceptions may be permitted and these are considered on their merit by the Duchy.

Principles and even detailed specifications are one thing, however, but in order to safeguard them through the entire implementation process there is a further link in the building chain. Throughout the process in which local architects prepare their plans and builders execute them, the Duchy retains control. This is achieved through a Building Agreement, whereby the freehold is only conveyed to the developer when the housing has been completed to the Duchy's satisfaction. Moreover, even at the point of transfer of the freehold, there is still a means of control over future changes initiated by residents. Every settlement evolves in its own way and, no matter how closely the original design is followed, the best of intentions can so easily be undone in the absence of continuing guidance. All residents thus receive from the Duchy a personal copy of the Poundbury Design Guidance, which shows in fine detail how proposed future changes should be managed.[18] The Prince of Wales himself has written a foreword to explain that the 'purpose of this guide is to identify the design principles which underlie Poundbury, and to indicate ways in which future alterations and extensions can enhance its character and appearance'.[19]

The guide itself, prepared by the architect planner Mervyn Miller, is directed to home-owners and their agents commissioned to undertake work that will affect the external appearance of a building. In the short history of Poundbury, such changes have included applications to build house extensions or fit ready-built conservatories, make loft conversions, infill car ports or install garden sheds. All such development requires the approval of either the Duchy or, subsequently, one of the dedicated management companies set up with resident representation. There are firm guidelines to assist an applicant, relating to such determinants as the visual impact not just on the street scene but on the view from the rear as well, the matching of materials to the original structure and a need to safeguard the privacy and amenity of neighbours. Other aspects of guidance relate to any proposed changes to building materials and architectural detailing, respect for principles of sustainability and walling materials.

A Question of Density

*'Anything above twelve houses per acre would be to build problems for the future: it was **town cramming** rather than **town planning**.'*[20]

The question of density has always been a divisive issue in planning new settlements. There is one school of thought that sees an opportunity to spread new homes more thinly than in the older cities; and another that espouses higher densities in the cause of good architecture and effective use of land.

From time to time, these differences surface around a live issue, as, indeed, is the case with Poundbury.

Poundbury is avowedly a high-density development, with an eventual gross density of some 20 persons per acre (assuming a target population of not less than 5000 over 250 acres of building land: another 150 acres will be devoted to a surrounding ring of green space). Under the banner of sustainability its tightly-packed houses and small gardens are part of a formula to make effective use of a relatively small area of land and to minimise journeys by car. To this is added the vogue of New Urbanist principles and the rhetoric of creating a sense of urban life and civic space; comparisons are made with the type of traditional European town that people like – namely, places with towers and public squares, with the security of a bustling street scene and with houses and workshops side by side.

As the experience of Poundbury illustrates, high-density development has influential advocates but, equally, it is by no means to everyone's taste. Foremost amongst the traditional advocates of lower densities is the Town and Country Planning Association, which throughout its long history has campaigned fiercely against high densities in greenfield development. The aim, it was argued, should be to free people from congested conditions and to respond to a natural preference for a house and garden. In response to criticism that the first garden cities (in the early 20th century) were not sufficiently 'urban', the pioneer town planner Raymond Unwin, joint designer with Barry Parker of Letchworth, wrote a book in 1912 with the telling title *Nothing Gained by Over-Crowding*. It was a title that remained over the years the watchword of the 'low density' campaigners. No-one was more fervent in defending this position than the Association's leading campaigner in the 1940s and 1950s, Frederic Osborn. He was constantly at war with what he saw as 'the tacit conspiracy between the countryside preservationists, the city authorities and the architects'.[21] Today the TCPA's vision is of a mix of densities: it supports concentrations of dwellings around public transport nodes at higher densities while continuing to argue for homes with gardens at lower densities elsewhere, particularly for families.

At the time of its inception, it is probably fair to conclude that more attention was focused on Poundbury's traditional architecture and unusual layout than on the more abstract idea of density. The first phase has, in any case, carried lower densities than more recent development, partly because of a lower rate of house occupancy. In later phases, the inclusion of larger family houses and a higher proportion of social housing has led to an increased number of people in a given area. Understandably, it is some of these newer residents who have objected most to continuing high-density development. This quite recent source of opposition is a product of the particular way in which Poundbury is evolving, being a mixture of initial master-planning and successive detailed planning applications. It was one thing at the end of the 1980s to win over the Dorchester community to the New Urbanist master-plan, and subsequently to build the first areas before a resident population became established. It is proving quite another matter to convince newcomers that the original principles should continue to be upheld. To many of these residents, the realisation of the underlying vision of Poundbury as a New Urbanist model counts for less than the aim of curbing further high-density development.

As an illustration of what is, perhaps, an endemic problem, things eventually came to a head in the late summer of 2004 around proposals for a site known as Jubilee Court. On the face of it this ought not to have been a matter of contention; the site was on one corner of cross-roads, the other three of which are already developed. In common with the principles of the master-plan this kind of location lends itself to an imposing form of development. Thus, diagonally opposite, there is a five-storey Italianate tower as part of a complex of offices and apartments, while the other two corner sites also contain landmark features. Jubilee Court was planned for 31 apartments and two shops in a mixture of five-, three- and two-storey buildings, together with car parking. The overall density proposed was variously assessed as 17 dwellings per acre by the local authority and 66 per acre by objectors, the difference depending on how much surrounding land one takes into account; the former figure compares with government guidelines which are now considerably higher than for traditional suburban housing.

Anticipating the prospect of opposition from neighbouring residents the local planning officer crafted a carefully researched report and recommended approval. His sense of trouble brewing was correct, and arguments were soon to be marshalled to oppose the application, with a campaign led by a professional town planner with a house overlooking the site. A lobbying group was formed with the acronym PROD, Poundbury Residents Opposed to Density. The group claimed that the density proposed could be compared with those of inner London housing estates. Although these claims were rejected by the local authority, at this point local politics kicked in and councillors on the planning committee proved chary of ignoring the interests of the 40 or so residents who came out in opposition to the scheme.

The application was duly rejected, as was, some months later, a revised scheme.[22]

There will be more cases like Jubilee Court, expressing a latent tension between the concept of a high-density settlement and the preference of residents, when really faced with a choice, to avoid the largely inevitable costs of this in the form of noise from neighbours, overlooking, obstructed views and an overspill of car parking. By reason of this unusual balance between, on the one hand, the Prince's vision and Leon Krier's master-plan and, on the other hand, the process of handing decisions on detailed development to local councillors, it will prove in the remaining phases increasingly difficult to maintain the essential principles of Poundbury.

Notes

1   John Ruskin, in Hardy (1979), p.79
2   Prince of Wales (1989), p.139
3   Extracts are from the 1994 Wordsworth Classics edition; the original novel was published in 1895
4   In Draper (2001), p.81
5   http://www.princeofwales.gov.uk/about/duc_poundbury.html
6   Thompson-Fawcett, M., 'Leon Krier and the organic revival within urban policy and practice', *Planning Perspectives*, Vol. 13, p.180. See also Butina-Watson (Report, 2004), in which the commissioning of consultants is discussed
7   The derivation of the word is interesting: with a different spelling, *charrette*, it refers to a two-wheeled cart in which French students in the late 19th century supposedly rushed their finished drawings to the Ecole des Beaux Arts in Paris to meet intentionally tight deadlines
8   C. Martin, in Miller, M., 'Poundbury, Dorchester: British New Urbanism or picturesque illusion?' Paper presented at the Tenth Biennial Conference on Planning History of the Society for American City and Regional Planning History, St Louis, Missouri, 6-9 November 2003
9   Leon Krier, 'The future of cities: the absurdity of modernism', 2001, http://www.planetizen.com.oped/item.php?id=35
10 Alan Baxter, *The Transactions of the Thursday Club*, No. 1, January 1992
11 Andres Duany, in Neal, ed. (2003), p.96
12 Murrain (Report, 2002), p.13
13 *Ibid.*, p.14
14 Krier, in Economakis, ed. (1992), p.25
15 The initial Building Code was prepared by Alan Baxter and Associates with input from Duany Plater-Zyberk
16 Murrain and Bolgar, in Commission for Architecture and the Built Environment (Report, 2004), p.37
17 *Building Code*, first version December 1994, reference made to revised version June 1999
18 Duchy of Cornwall, *Poundbury Design Guidance*, commissioned by the Duchy and written by Mervyn Miller
19 *Ibid.*
20 Discussion of Frederic Osborn's campaign against high densities in the 1950s, in Hardy (1991), p.50
21 Osborn, in a letter to Lewis Mumford, 29 January 1952
22 An appeal was subsequently lodged by the developer but was not upheld on matters of detail

Chapter 4

Building in Style

'He builded better than he knew,
The conscious stone to beauty grew.' [1]

Whether one loves it or loathes it, Poundbury is certainly different from run-of-the-mill development elsewhere. Some elements are not necessarily unique, but there is nothing to compare with the scale of the Poundbury experiment. On entering the new settlement one can be in no doubt that it is planned and built on the basis of a set of principles consciously conceived to do something new. Confronted with a picturesque townscape, visitors invariably ask whether they have stepped back in time, or is this the future?

Enter the Builders

'Absolutely fundamental to the whole Poundbury idea is a belief
in true quality. That means using proper materials in the proper way.' [2]

In selecting its builders the Duchy has favoured (but not exclusively so) local family firms with a reputation for traditional excellence. Tenders are issued for

Poundbury in the making

particular parcels of development and the award of subsequent contracts is linked directly to performance to date. Two Dorset firms, C.G. Fry & Son and Morrish Builders, have played major roles in Phase 1 and more recently in Phase 2; in the latter they have been joined by a nationally based firm, Westbury. There is also scope for selected local firms to bid for smaller contracts, typically for infill development.

The process can be illustrated through the experience of one of these firms, C.G. Fry & Son of Litton Cheney. The picturesque village, in rolling countryside midway between Dorchester and Bridport, where the firm's head office is based might seem an unlikely location for an innovative building firm. In fact, the rural setting is why it is here in the first place, for this is a Dorset firm with a long history in the area. Its origins are based on various crafts associated with building, and over time these traditional activities have been adapted effectively to the challenge of new technologies and changing demands. For several centuries the Fry family has had a presence in the village, first as wheelwrights and, through their joinery skills (following a pattern that was familiar in rural society), also as coffin-makers and undertakers. It was not until the 1920s that the then head of the business, Charles George Fry, branched into general building and established the present firm. This embedded history explains why (unlike many firms that now prefer to use sub-contractors) there is still a joinery workshop to support its building contracts.

Philip Fry, the current Managing Director, represents the third generation of this family firm and is respectful of its long traditions. In explaining how the business became involved in Poundbury, he recalls his father taking him at the end of the 1980s to an exhibition in Dorchester showing the very first plans for the proposed settlement. At the time, it all seemed rather fanciful to young Philip but his father immediately saw the potential and declared, then and there, that C.G. Fry & Son would play an important role in making it all happen. It was already well placed to do so, with wide experience of working in the Dorset vernacular in both new development and the restoration of period homes. With some pride, before Poundbury set new standards, it could point to the success of a newly completed scheme in the nearby village of Abbotsbury, where attractive modern houses had been built in a traditional idiom. The Prince of Wales was quick to acknowledge the quality of the Abbotsbury scheme, which he duly opened, and in so doing gave a strong signal of the kind of building he hoped to see in his own project.

When it came to inviting tenders for the initial phase of new housing on the Poundbury site, C.G. Fry won the first contract, for 65 houses, and has been on site ever since. The nature of the process has changed over the years, and Philip Fry recalls that the guidance for the first development was totally prescriptive. In contrast, the more that the various parties could trust each other and learn from shared experience the more flexible the process became. Typically, while more recent development continues to be guided by Leon Krier's master-plan and his specifications for the likes of plot sizes, plot ratios and building lines to define the street scene, it is now left much more for the builder to interpret the Poundbury Building Code and apply it to the area in question. C.G. Fry commissions its own architects from an approved panel, mainly locally based, and presents a draft scheme to the Duchy. The plans are then scrutinised by four key people: Leon Krier, the master-planner; the Consultant Architect, David Oliver; the Development Director, Andrew Hamilton; and the Prince himself, who takes a very active interest in the detailed designs.

Only when they have overcome this process can the builders submit their plans to the local authority for planning approval.

With these various procedures complete, work at last starts on site. Philip Fry is keen to acknowledge the skills of his own site manager in interpreting the plans and making minor adaptations where these prove necessary to meet variations in materials or fittings produced off site. He is also full of praise for the various craftsmen who by now are familiar with the style required and have to make their own day-to-day modifications. When asked to identify the key to making the process work and producing the right outcomes, he is in no doubt that 'attention to detail' is the answer. For C.G. Fry, as for the other builders, the Poundbury Building Code is a constant source of reference and each of the builders will have a well-thumbed copy in their office.

Repeatedly, when trying to understand how Poundbury is achieving consistency, respondents share the same conclusion, namely that the whole process has been well thought through and no effort is spared to attend to every detail. There is also a ready acknowledgement that quality has to be a hallmark of the building at every stage, and of the importance of a common respect for tradition. In its own promotional literature, for instance, C.G. Fry claims a reputation based on traditional style, 'always sympathetic to the local surroundings yet offering the best of current building technology';[3] in the words of Leon Krier this is being modern without subscribing to modernism.

Building Sustainably

*'There have been so many false dawns when it comes to promoting
more sustainable housing that any optimism today may seem unwise.
But it's hard not to feel optimistic looking at the way trends are
now moving.'* [4]

It has taken a long time in coming but governments and the development industry have finally woken up to the need to build today's settlements with an eye on tomorrow. Global warming, limited oil reserves, regional water shortages and diminishing supplies of finite resources are all warning signals that can no longer be ignored. The belated, and still partial, response is to encourage a new approach under the general banner of sustainability. In the United States the term 'smart growth' is also used, in the wider sense of preventing urban sprawl and pollution, and reducing the profligate use of non-renewable fuels, particularly an excessive dependency on the use of private cars.[5]

Particularly at a time of rapid housing expansion, the design of new homes is a critical element in the present drive to hold back global warming and reduce demands on scarce resources; for instance, 27 per cent of carbon dioxide emissions in the UK comes from the housing sector. There are now examples of good practice where new houses use renewable energy technologies and achieve zero carbon emissions, where water is efficiently recycled and where non-renewable building materials are used sparingly if at all. Although the planning laws and building regulations are generally regarded as not being geared sufficiently to actively promote sustainable development, it remains possible for individual and localised initiatives to do so.

Thus, in the case of Poundbury, the various builders are required to meet, at the very least, minimum environmental standards in support of sustainability and are expected to go beyond these where possible. A common requirement is that all of the buildings have to be constructed of traditional, heavyweight materials that, in themselves, are energy efficient. Typically, in cold weather such buildings have the effect of storing solar energy in the day and releasing it into the rooms at night; likewise on hot days the interior can remain relatively cool. As a rule of thumb, 'a well-designed passive building will be at about the mean temperature between the outdoor mean maximum and the outdoor mean minimum'.[6]

The extent to which all of this is actually achieved is quantified through the application of what is generally regarded as the industry standard, known by the acronym BREEAM (Building Research Establishment Environmental Assessment Method). Buildings are assessed at the design stage to evaluate their anticipated environmental impact, and credits are awarded against different criteria to demonstrate whether the buildings will surpass the minimum requirements of standard building regulations. If sufficient credits are accumulated a BREEAM certificate is awarded, and a record of all such assessments is maintained by the Duchy.

Criteria for assessment are grouped into three categories, relating in turn to the global, local and indoor environment. For instance, in order to get points in the first category, new buildings must be designed to minimise carbon dioxide greenhouse gas emissions from fossil fuel burning. This can be achieved through sufficiently effective wall, roof and floor insulation, and through double- or triple-glazing, low-emissivity glass and draught-sealing. Under the second category, in relation to the local environment, criteria include use of sustainable timber, water economy measures and extensive use of recycled building materials. Finally, indoor features are measured in terms of the likes of controlled ventilation and heat recovery systems, avoidance of the use of asbestos and lead-based paints, and extractor fans in kitchens to remove possible pollutants.

Although beyond the remit of BREEAM, there are other aspects of a town's development that can contribute to the overall level of sustainability. For instance, what use can be made of renewable energy and local energy sources; what methods are adopted for waste management; how is pollution and waste controlled during construction and demolition; what thought is given to subsequent pollution control (such as air quality, noise and light pollution); how is biodiversity and landscape protection promoted; what has been done to conserve and manage water resources; and, finally, to what extent is account taken of some of the health and social impacts of design and layout?

To different degrees these issues are acknowledged in Poundbury, but even in a place that seeks to be innovative the response is far from exhaustive. Only in a relatively few cases is there a clear attempt to extend into pioneering territory; the work of one developer, Kim Slowe, is particularly noteworthy.[7]

Kim Slowe is one of life's entrepreneurs, making light of challenges that would deter others. When he left the Royal Navy, where he served as a helicopter pilot and frigate captain, his first intention was to set up an on-line rental service for holiday cottages. He also had a keen interest in alternative therapies and it was that interest which led him, indirectly, into a thriving development business. Having persuaded the Duchy of the need for a dedicated holistic clinic, he then took on the job of building it. Fortunately, he was able to call on the help of two cousins already in the building trade, who let him make use of an existing company structure, Cornhill Estates. Starting this work at the age of 42, the clinic was to be his first building in Poundbury, but when it was completed, instead of moving directly on to other development projects, he spent the following year in building up the new practice. This is now an established part of Poundbury life.

Helped by the success of this first project, Kim later won further Poundbury tenders, boldly taking on difficult sites that other builders preferred to avoid. One of these was an unpromising strip of land opposite a factory site, where he pioneered a terrace of inventive 'eco' houses. His aim here was quite simply to advance the cause of sustainability and, at the same time, to demonstrate that sound ecological structures need not be instantly recognisable because of wind pumps on the roof and compost silos in the front garden. Instead, he built an elegant terrace that would not be out of

Terrace of 'eco' houses in Peverell Avenue East

place in a Bath crescent, yet containing within it some of the most advanced energy conservation techniques. The owners themselves are appreciative of low energy bills resulting from techniques such as solar heating (by means of sealed vacuum tubes), sheep wool loft insulation, thin mortar between building blocks to reduce heat loss, and wall insulation that is double the normal specification.

Against all the odds, these houses were sold as soon as they came onto the market, confounding those critics who believed that the public was not yet willing to pay for the extra costs of sustainable technology. He is also bucking a trend based on fears that the very high cost of some alternative technologies will push up building costs and effectively reduce land values. Undeterred, Kim Slowe is currently planning a further 'eco' scheme in Poundbury as well as larger developments in other parts of the country.

A Walk Around Poundbury

'Every detail in this honey-coloured development is aimed at pleasing the eye, in contrast to the suburban sprawl which has characterized much of post-war planning.' [8]

We have all become so used to the failings of modern development that, as some visitors remark, when something is done that sets new standards it almost 'doesn't seem real'. What they really mean is that Poundbury is clearly not at all like the typical, dreary estates that are attached to most British cities. To make the point, there is nothing more telling than to take a walk through the streets and squares of Poundbury, following the tracks of an estimated 30,000 visitors a year.

Daniel Silk is a local resident who (amongst other entrepreneurial ventures) has produced an attractive, axonometric representation of Poundbury that is much appreciated by residents and visitors alike. Clutching a copy of this map, a natural starting point is Pummery Square, at the heart of Phase 1. The gravelled square is quintessential Poundbury, a stage set of traditional styles and communal facilities. On one side is Brownsword Hall, a high gabled structure raised on columns, not unlike an old granary or wool barn, to provide a sheltered space at ground floor level. Sponsored by Andrew

Brownsword Hall, in Pummery Square

Clockwise from top left: the Octagon Café, Poundbury Village Stores, and the Poet Laureate pub

Brownsword, the greetings card magnate, and completed in 1999, the building would not be out of place in a town square in France or central Europe, serving not just as an architectural focus but also as a community hub. Leon Krier wanted to see a tower as part of this building and retains hopes of achieving this through a later addition.

On the other three sides of the square is a mix of shops and the Poundbury pub, the 'Poet Laureate', with a portrait of Ted Hughes on the sign board. The building itself is essentially Georgian with a distinctly maritime flavour – the kind of place one would find on nearby Weymouth's harbour front – and was originally planned to include hotel accommodation. On an adjoining side is a colonnaded walkway that frames the village store – a national franchise, Budgens, its design tempered discreetly to meet local requirements. Just off the main square is the Octagon Café, an attractive space modelled as a

Holmead Walk

Georgian conservatory and ever popular as an informal meeting point. Both the neighbouring pub and the café set tables and chairs outside in a piazza environment, creating even more of a continental ambience for the square.

If one is to walk south from the square, the vista closes on what looks like a small Greek temple, sited at the edge of the settlement; closer inspection reveals that this is a folly to conceal an electricity sub-station. Bearing west at this point is the start of Holmead Walk, a line of elegant, tall houses, some part-brick and others wholly white rendered, of essentially Georgian architecture, grand in appearance and providing a dramatic edge to Poundbury. One of the buildings emulates an early chapel, of the kind one might find in a New England township, but there were no takers to use it, as intended, as a place of worship; instead, it is now occupied in part by a retail store for sound systems and in part as an apartment.

Holmead Walk is true 'edge' development, overlooking a mixture of playing areas and farmland (with a flock of sheep invariably in place to add to the bucolic atmosphere) and a splendid view of Maiden Castle beyond. Along this peripheral road (which remains largely unmade to discourage through-traffic) there are cleverly placed archways to create added interest, and one can follow the narrow walkways through these into the streets and squares beyond. Chaseborough Square, for instance, is a quiet residential enclave with a mixture of styles that includes an eye-catching house with Dutch gables. In the middle of the square is a fountain, a feature much favoured by New Urbanist architects.

Above: Chaseborough Square
Right: Brookhouse Street
Below: Middlemarsh Street and Fleur de Lis

Returning to Pummery Square, one can follow the route of Brookhouse Street (the term 'street' is preferred to more suburban descriptors to convey a sense of urban living – no Acacia Avenues in Poundbury), a narrow, curved street that is closed to traffic. Terraced cottages line the gravelled path and a couple of trees are planted down the middle. Alternatively, one can take a northward direction from the main square, into one of the earliest developments, Middlemarsh Street. This is an iconic street that sets the tone for the whole development, conveying an unmistakeable impression of a thoroughfare in a traditional market town. On one of the 'historic' cottages is a plaque to show the actual date of building, 1994. At the head of that street is one of Poundbury's signature buildings, the *Fleur de Lis* retirement apartments, distinguished by two tall towers, one conical and the other pyramidal. These are known locally as the 'Disney towers' or, even less ceremoniously, 'Madonna's bra'.

Partly because the residents have bonded over their ten years or so of occupation and partly because of a more relaxed layout with slightly lower densities than later development, Phase 1 has been branded by its residents as 'Poundbury Village' (distinguishing it from all that follows). The brand (although potentially divisive) is not without justification as it undoubtedly has more of the feel of a village than a town. In contrast, Phase 2 tends to be higher density, is more urban in character and, to date, lacks the mature vegetation in the gardens and streets that softens the impact of the earlier phase of development.

Like Phase 1, however, this more recent and (at the time of writing) ongoing development has its own landmark buildings and squares. With the *Fleur de Lis* now to the rear, walking west along the Bridport Road (if the master-plan is to be followed, soon to be re-routed along a new parkway skirting the south of Poundbury) the start of Phase 2 is marked by two imposing buildings on either side of the main road. One is a nursing and residential home and the other a complex of apartments, together with a beauty salon and offices to the rear. Although the styles are contrasting, the shared height and sense of grandeur of the two buildings provide a strong sense of entrance to a different part of Poundbury. The nursing home rises to five storeys, like a sentinel tower overlooking the Bridport Road, with the rest of it generally three storeys; good use has been made of local stone. Designed by James Gorst, an *aficionado* of Arts and Crafts, its style is certainly not out of a conventional pattern book and might best be described as 'German monastic'. In contrast, the apartment block is classic 18th-century Palladian, rendered in white and with a formal lawn along the frontage. Four pilasters are built into the upper two storeys, appearing to support a pediment above. Unlike its authentic forebears the hidden structure is formed of concrete

blocks, although looking none the less grand in its finished form.

Skirting to the south of Poundbury's Palladian landmark, one follows Middle Farm Way, the route of the proposed parkway. In anticipation of through-traffic, the present road is wider than elsewhere, with generous grass verges planted with trees. The houses themselves offer a mixture

Two imposing buildings mark the start of Phase 2

Views from Middle Farm Way, including, above, a gargoyle put in place to obscure a gas flue

of styles but all of them eye-catching in their way. Perhaps the most unusual is the one fashioned after a pink castle, with its narrow arched windows and leadwork; to one side a potentially offending gas flue has been obscured by a gargoyle, hissing steam instead of water. Further along is the site of the former Middle Farm barn and other buildings, now carefully restored and used for a variety of purposes, including a veterinary clinic. The Duchy itself until recently made use of the old farmhouse for its own offices, before moving to a more central location, in the former house of Poundbury Farm.

Making one's way further into Phase 2, along Netherton Street, one sees an interesting variety of building styles, both domestic and commercial, all modelled on actual buildings in this part of Dorset. At the far end of that street is a large unit that accommodates the chocolate factory, and then the first of two squares in this latest phase of development. The centrepoint of this square is an ornamental fountain with bronze figures in a classical mould; it was

donated by a developer, Derek Newell, and made in Dorset's Cranborne Forge. On two sides there is an uninterrupted view from the houses and apartments, but it is also very much a public venue. The square fronts Bridport Road, and the junction is seen as another location where a few impressive buildings can impart a sense of place: an Italianate tower on one corner, a colonnaded block of offices on another, and a tasteful art gallery on a third corner. Although the remaining corner has yet to be filled, the plans are for something with sufficient height and density to mark an important thoroughfare.

Nearby, on the far side of Bridport Road, is Whitecross Square, where an opportunity has been lost for more generous tree planting and a real sense of place. Beyond that is

Above: A classical bronze fountain and Italianate tower in Victor Jackson Avenue

Below: Varied house styles in Moraston Street

Octagonal house and flint cottages in Moraston Street

much of the newer building, quite tightly packed but with an interesting variety of styles and spaces. Along Moraston Street, for instance, is a very distinctive octagonal house and then a row of attractive flint cottages, followed, in turn, by a cluster of Regency and Victorian town houses. Leaving Whitecross Square in a different direction one can work one's way through a choice of alleys and yards before reaching a classic crescent development facing a copse of mature trees (complete with a lively rookery in the top branches), forming the grounds of what used to be the Poundbury Farm buildings. Residents there have likened the crescent to what one might find in Bath. In the former barns there are plans for a garden centre.

Wherever one walks in Poundbury it is tempting to wander through some of the courtyards, designed mainly for garage access and off-street parking but also with their own trees and planting pockets. This is an important feature and it has been claimed that 'what makes Poundbury so appealing to residents and visitors alike, is the way its highly individual properties are all arranged in mews, squares and courtyards, creating attractive streetscapes wherever you look.'[9] To try to avoid the problem of misuse of these areas there is often a house or two facing into the yard, and residents are not slow to report any possible misdemeanour.

Returning eastwards, the route follows what will become the second important thoroughfare (the first being the southern parkway), Peverell Avenue East. New Urbanists like to emphasise frontage development, and here the distinctive style is white rendered Georgian three-storey houses, many with porches and external stairs and railings. Not that Peverell Avenue East is solely residential, with the inclusion of two large factories and a publishing

Peverell Avenue East

house, and on the largely undeveloped side of the road a proposed leisure centre and park complete with cricket field. It is unlikely that the intention to create a grand avenue will be fully achieved until suitable tree planting reaches maturity.

Throughout the scheme one cannot but be impressed by the careful detailing in each building and the attractive range of materials that has been used; where possible the latter is sourced from local quarries, although there are also some far-flung imports (kerb stone from China, patio stonework from India and grey slates from Spain). Eve Stephens is a Poundbury resident who has made a study of the stone used in its building, publishing her findings in a book, *Walking with Dinosaurs in Poundbury: A Geological Description of the Stone Houses*.[10] As an author with a keen interest in geology, her fascination is with the use of local stone. She explains, for instance, how the cream coloured columns supporting Brownsword Hall are made from Bath stone, a Jurassic limestone renowned for its fine texture and strength. In the same building, the plinths and door are shaped from Ham stone, a darker material that is quarried at Ham Hill, to the west of Yeovil. This, too, is limestone but a golden brown rather than cream in colour. In turn, the flagstones around the building are sourced from the Isle of Purbeck and are known locally as Downsvein; Portland stone in its different forms is used widely throughout Poundbury, although it was found not to be as effective for kerbstone as imported varieties. Looking ahead to the later phases of development, Eve Stephens points out that there will be a more sparing use of stone in construction, something to be regretted as its generous use in the first phase has been an important source of its character.

The design of street furniture is also of an unusually high standard, although here and there the bureaucratic powers of highway engineers and bye-laws challenge the quiet order of the street scene. Even though there is generally a good rapport with the county's highway engineers, sometimes, with the best will in the world, the regulations are simply too inflexible to adapt.[11] Roundabouts, for instance, are not amongst Poundbury's most acclaimed features, starkly landscaped and dominated by conventional directional signs in duplicate. In the case of the design and positioning of street lamps the record is very much better. Sometimes, street lamps are mounted on wall brackets, designed to cast pools of light without interfering with one's views of the night sky. The lighting also illustrates an interesting example of conflict between architectural preference and consumer choice; some of the lighting emits a yellow glow while the rest is white. In drawing up his plans, Leon Krier was unequivocal in advocating the latter on the grounds that 'the orange-amber of sodium vapours eliminates colours, flattens contrasts, destroys character and bathes even the most beautiful place in standardised gloom' whereas 'white lighting, on the other hand, has advantages from the point of view of both security and aesthetics'.[12] In spite of this advocacy, the mixed response in the streets of Poundbury reflects different management decisions, with some groups arguing (without foundation) that yellow lights are more economical.

Carefully designed street lighting

Other aspects of the street scene are no less carefully considered. Street signs and house numbering are discreet in the form of uniformly raised lettering and numbering, white on black, and the colours of front doors are all derived from approved palettes. Television aerials and satellite dishes are absent from view as a result of hidden communal receivers and underground cabling. Perhaps the most noticeable difference, though, compared with conventional schemes, is the welcome absence of superfluous signs and yellow lines on the roadway; some signs seem to be inevitable, but these, at least, have been kept to a minimum. At a time when there are national campaigns to remove the clutter of

Courtyards and alleys are an attractive and well-used feature

signs that ruin the appearance of so many of Britain's cities, the example of Poundbury is a lesson that is well worth taking.

Walking through the streets of Poundbury and cutting through the various courtyards and alleys is itself testimony to a design that is intended to encourage people to get around without their car; doing so is both possible and pleasant. Good layout design is one thing, but changing the habit of a lifetime is quite another. Even in a place like Poundbury, where there is a conscious attempt to break the mould, many choose to follow the old ways. Each morning and afternoon children are carried in the back of a car to and from the nearby schools; many of those who live locally still choose to drive to work; and cars draw up outside the village store to allow their owners to buy a daily newspaper. A survey of user satisfaction confirms that the care that has been put into the layout to encourage less use of the car 'has made little immediate difference to residents' overall patterns of travel to work or to shop'.[13] With higher fuel prices in the future this pattern may well change, and the radical layout that has been put in place will enable it to do so.

Notes

1   Ralph Waldo Emerson, 'The Snowstorm'
2   C.G.Fry & Son, promotional leaflet
3   *Ibid.*
4   Jonathon Porritt, in TCPA (Report, 2003)
5   http://www.wordiq.com/definition/Smart_Growth
6   Butina-Watson *et al.* (Report, 2004), p.39
7   Interview with Kim Slowe, 14 March 2005
8   Tracey Harrison, *Daily Mail*, in C.G. Fry & Son promotional brochure, *Poundbury, Dorchester*
9   C.G. Fry & Son promotional leaflet
10   First published in January 2004, the book is self-published and available locally in Poundbury outlets
11   Interview with Ian Madgwick and his colleague, Dave Brown, Dorset County Council, 24 January 2005. Clearly, there has been a positive approach to finding ways to meet the special needs of Poundbury. A useful source of reference is the County Council's publication, *Highway Guidance for Estate Roads*, 2002
12   Krier (1998), p.167
13   Butina-Watson *et al.* (Report, 2004), p.32

Chapter 5

Pocket Handkerchief Gardens

'Gardens are about as small as they can get without the residents beginning to feel deprived.'[1]

Gardens in Poundbury are small: in fact, generally very small. There are none of the 100-foot gardens here that are taken for granted in suburbia. This difference is the key to Poundbury remaining a compact settlement; small plots are essential if everything is to be within walking distance. Houses and garages are no smaller than anywhere else, and road widths are regulated by the highway engineers. But the size of garden plots is discretionary and it's here that the Duchy has been able to pack it all in.

Digging for Britain

'... the small garden, by existing in such enormous numbers, has become the key to a much improved quality of life in these small islands, on this small planet.'[2]

We are, if the various surveys are to be believed, a nation of gardeners; on a fine summer's day, contends the garden historian Jenny Uglow, across the country 'we are out in the garden'.[3] Tending one's garden is the number one leisure pursuit. Whether pruning roses or lounging on a sun deck, fitting a water feature or mowing the lawn, we are drawn into our gardens for a variety of reasons. Growing one's own vegetables remains a popular pastime but no longer the economic necessity that was once the main justification of a plot of land around one's house. Instead, gardens are more likely to be seen as an opportunity to exercise one's creative talents, or simply as somewhere to relax; a place of aesthetic appreciation, or one of gentle repose. Increasingly, gardens have become a means of displaying one's wealth, if not a mere fashion accessory – an outdoor room with carefully selected décor. Gardens to re-create a wilderness or for cottage flowers, for a cluster of herbs or diminutive alpine transplants; more functionally, a place to kick a ball or gather round a barbecue. Or, perhaps, a home for ponds and rose trellises, patios and pergolas, containers and raised beds. And when the intrepid gardener is not admiring their self-made place in the sun there's always the garden centre for an afternoon trip, or a succession of television programmes urging one to be ever more adventurous, until the very sameness of it all induces monotony.

The present trend in gardening is driven partly by more leisure time (for those at work as well as amongst the burgeoning population of retirees) and also by greater disposable income. For the traditional gardener taking cuttings and growing prize leeks, the garden needn't be a drain on one's purse, but for the modern gardener it can be the most expensive room in the house. Ironically, this trend towards a more extravagant use of one's plot is taking place at a time when gardens are getting smaller. Even in recent history the pattern was very different.

In the heyday of suburban expansion before the Second World War, houses were commonly laid out at 12 to the acre and developers would not have dreamt of trying to market one of their *bijou* residences without a respectable sized garden. In some of the 'up market' developments it would not have been uncommon to see gardens of up to 300 feet in length. The historian of suburban London, Alan A. Jackson, shows how important were gardens, front and back, to the new occupiers. 'Well groomed gardens were seen everywhere in the new suburbs, an outlet for creative drives suppressed in the routines of office life; many of the new house owners devoted almost all their leisure daylight hours to them, growing vegetables and fruit as well as mounting a floral display for nine months of the year.'[4]

This was also the time of the first suburban council housing estates, and there, too, it was expected that a decent sized garden would be provided. On the whole, though, concludes Jackson, 'the gardens received less care and attention, fewer trees and shrubs were planted, and the streets and house surrounds were frequently left untidy and unkempt'.[5] Gardens, as in other aspects of housing, reflect social divisions as well as a commonality of interest.

During the Second World War, with supplies of imported food cut off by enemy shipping, many of the nation's gardens were converted into vegetable plots and it was not uncommon, too, to bring in a few hens and maybe even a pig. 'Dig for Victory' was a popular catchphrase and an encouragement to those on the home front to make their own contribution to the war effort. Amongst the leaflets produced by the Ministry of Information to inspire a sense of patriotism through digging one's plot were 'The Garden Goes to War' and 'Cloches versus Hitler'.

In the years that followed, new gardens have become progressively smaller. During the 1950s, with the memory of wartime food shortages still in people's minds, there was a reluctance to take out of agriculture more land than was absolutely necessary. Building land was, therefore, at a premium and land was not used needlessly for private gardens. The agricultural economist Robin Best argued at the time that this was not a sensible course to follow as, in his calculations, domestic gardens were actually likely to be more productive than the same acreage of farmland. On this basis, to maximise food production, it would have been better to provide larger rather than smaller gardens.[6]

Best's advice was not heeded. Even, or perhaps especially, in the post-war new towns (successors to the pioneer garden cities where ample sized plots were a much admired feature), house plots were compact. By the 1960s, the food argument had been largely forgotten and the dictates of land economics reduced the size of plots still further, although by present standards the gardens at that time would still seem quite adequate. The fact is that the size of a garden is relative, and 'small' gardens for an earlier generation might seem very generous today. In 1952, the first edition appeared of C.E. Lucas Philips's *The Small Garden*, written to meet the needs of those who owned a small garden, defined as having 'a limit of about an acre, but with special consideration for the suburban garden of less than half that size'.[7]

Lucas Philips was a retired brigadier whose notion of a small garden was not shared by a new generation of house-owners. More in tune with modern developments, John Brookes broke fresh ground in 1969 with the telling title *The Room Outside*. Brookes was a designer by background who had travelled widely in Europe and the United States and was attracted especially by some of the modernist gardens he saw in California. The small garden, he argued, should be treated in the words of the title of his book, as an extra room outdoors. He put a new emphasis on texture, pattern and colour in fences and paving and advocated more use of hard landscaping. As well as relatively cheap, mass produced materials he encouraged a search for discovered objects, just as one scatters such ornaments in internal rooms. In 1985 he published a follow-up book, *The Small Garden*, using exactly the same title as that of Lucas Philips but to tell of a very different concept.

Recognising the extent of the contemporary market, there is now a plethora of such publications in the bookshops, dispensing ideas on how to lay out imaginatively what have become quite tiny parcels of land. Anthony Noel, for instance, is a former actor who has written a book, *Great Little Gardens*, in which he brings the drama of the stage into the most unlikely of spaces. For owners of small gardens he writes encouragingly that 'a garden does not have to be large for you to make the most of perspective, space and scale: it is possible to create bold vistas and outlines even in a tiny area'.[8] In another book on this theme, *Small Gardens*, Peter McHoy uses his own back garden, measuring nine metres square (not untypical of many Poundbury gardens) to illustrate his various ideas and designs. And he reminds his readers that a small garden has its own advantages: being easier to maintain than a large one and less expensive to lay out and plant.

To leave the reader in no doubt of the scale of the topic, Jill Billington (writing for the Royal Horticultural Society) entitles her book *Really Small Gardens*. Her key message is that in very small gardens everything counts, and meticulous planning is, therefore, essential. Such gardens should be planned as a simplified whole and an intimate expression of the owner. From a trans-Atlantic perspective, Keith Davitt, in *Small Spaces: Beautiful Gardens*, believes that small gardens are too often neglected because their owners fail to realise the potential of limited areas. He offers a series of designs that seek to exploit unified themes in small spaces: like an English cottage garden or a Japanese meditation sanctuary, a water garden or a modern combination of stone patio and luxuriant plants.

Through these joint efforts, coupled with the impact of television and other media, there is now a growing acceptance of small gardens that might in an earlier day have been considered as little more than backyards. With good design it is shown that these spaces can be every bit as attractive as a larger garden, even if the variety one finds in the latter is, inevitably, missing. Moreover, in spite of an almost universal love of gardens, many people are either unwilling or unable to devote too much time or effort to their maintenance; in these cases, small plots can be seen as a virtue.

'Look for the Green Ribbons'

'All gardens serve the purpose of the people who make them. They are part of the lifestyle which everyone creates... a garden is a social statement and a declaration of the owner's taste.' [9]

Once a year, on a Sunday in June, out come the straw hats and floaty dresses as the residents of Poundbury take part in the annual Open Gardens Day. Green ribbons are tied to the gate posts to signal which of the gardens are open to visitors. Everyone is invited to open their garden and doubters are

reminded that the day is not about 'perfect gardens'; rather it is planned as an opportunity to share ideas and to see what can be done with what are initially quite unpromising plots. As very few people have been resident for more than ten years it is also a chance to encourage newcomers who wonder if their plot of building rubble with a thin layer of topsoil can ever mature into a place of beauty and enjoyment.

In spite of the reassuring plea that it should not be just about 'perfect gardens', it does tend to be the owners who are more confident of their achievements who respond to the invitation. That is no bad thing in itself, for the visitor is presented with what is in effect a living exhibition of small garden design and maintenance. Given the relative uniformity and unpromising characteristics of the initial plots, the results are remarkably diverse and enterprising. In some (although really quite a minority) one comes across an uncompromising homage to modernism: geometric stone slabs laid across each other in a cruciform structure, with water trickling across the surfaces from a hidden source, and carefully chosen shrubs of a distinctly spiky nature. In others, Poundbury's theme of an old market town is

enthusiastically picked up, with cottage gardens filled with delphiniums and rambling roses, brightly coloured poppies and clumps of scabious, orange marigolds and delicate fritillaries.

Patios are universal and conservatories are popular as a means of extending the living room into the garden, or purely as an extension for space-hungry children. Water features, an icon of fashion, are also much in evidence, with fountains mounted on the surrounding walls and ponds sited centrally at the heart of the garden design. Another feature of the contemporary small garden is the use made of metal or stone sculptures and different forms of artwork. Because so many gardens are overlooked, use is made of climbing evergreens to provide a constant screen, with trellises mounted along the tops of walls and fences to secure at least a modicum of privacy.

New residents complain of the paucity of bird life but are reassured by those who have been in Poundbury for longer that the birds, driven away during the period of intensive building, will soon return. With the help of nesting boxes, bird baths and feeding tables this is the case, and most gardens can record the presence of a reasonable variety of species. Blackbirds fill the air with birdsong, and swallows make their miraculous return from a winter in the sun to pick out former nesting places; perky wagtails are popular residents, and robins and wrens are quick to explore new feeding opportunities. A single clump of mature trees in the centre of Poundbury is home to a noisy rookery, and seagulls drawn in from the nearby coast add to the high-level screeches. These larger birds as well as smaller species make good use of the ubiquitous chimney tops, perching there safe from predators while they take stock of their surroundings.

Meanwhile, at ground level, most houses front directly onto the street, with typically little more than a planting pocket along the front elevation or a narrow strip behind metal railings. Certainly, there is nothing to compare with traditional suburban front gardens in Britain or the lawn alongside a driveway that is more typical in the United States. In spite of very limited

planting possibilities, most residents have managed to pack in lavender and rosemary, climbing roses and pyracantha, to lend colour and texture to the street scene. Some of these diminutive front gardens are, indeed, works of art in their own right.

The very smallness of the gardens has encouraged ingenuity and effective use of every inch available. People have risen to the challenge and sanctuaries have been created in what must have seemed at first the most unlikely of places. While many people would like to have more space, there is a reasonably high level of satisfaction with what is provided.[10] Indeed, for some, the prospect of a small garden was one of the reasons for coming to Poundbury; previously owners of large plots, they are no longer willing or able to devote so much of their time to gardening on that scale.

The story of Arthur and Yvette Smith is not untypical. After a career for Arthur in the Civil Service that led to frequent house moves, and a subsequent period of retirement, the couple decided that it was time to 'down-size'. In 2004 they moved from south Devon to a cottage in Poundbury, one of the attractions being its small and manageable garden. Previously, they had struggled with two lawn-mowers; now they decided to commission a landscape architect to design their outdoor space with labour saving in mind. The result is an appealing hard landscape using a variety of screes and pebbles;

Arthur jokingly likens it to a piece of Chesil Beach. It is wholly a place to enjoy, without the burden of having to work too hard to maintain it.

Poundbury's new gardens have also proved to be a source of new business opportunities. Daniel Silk, for instance, showed initiative in starting a garden maintenance service, and his yellow van was, until recently, regularly sighted around the town.[11] Even though gardens are small there is a ready demand for someone to water the plants and keep the weeds down while owners are away. Local landscape architects have also benefited from commissions to convert barren plots into places of delight. Finally, and none too soon, a well established firm of Dorset garden centres is set to open a new centre in 2006, to be located amongst the former barns of Poundbury Farm.

Gardens in Poundbury are widely valued for what they are and are a frequent source of conversation and exchange of ideas. Although times have moved on and circumstances are different now, the words of one of the leading garden city pioneers, C.B. Purdom, written in 1913 about the role of the gardens in helping to cement the character of the then new garden city of Letchworth, are worth recalling:

'However various our occupations and tastes, however conflicting our opinions, in the garden we are united. There we find a common interest; there we have the same enemies and join in one battle, and aim after a single perfection. A community brought together by such means will, in the development of its social consciousness, acquire the strong qualities of mind and body which will fit it to undertake experiment and adventure, without which our common life becomes stagnant. The occupations of the garden provide excellent training for the world and the government of affairs. They add to dignity and self-confidence, and cause men to think well of themselves. A gardener has the caution that reformers lack. He knows that while great things come from small beginnings, a goodly tree does not spring up in one night; that what quickly grows as quickly perishes. He knows how complex and variable is nature and how utterly we are in her hands. He will know, if others forget it, that the building of a Garden City will not be the work of one day.'[12]

In a modern context, there is, however, an important cultural issue that is respectfully considered by the author of the seminal book on council housing, Alison Ravetz. She points out that in early council housing it was expected that pride would be taken in gardens, and cites the example of tenants in the new Becontree estate in the 1920s, who were exhorted to 'keep your house clean and your gardens tidy. Make them the envy of your neighbours...'[13] It was commonplace to read reports of exemplary gardens on council estates, and an acceptance of regulations that often extended to keeping one's washing out of sight of passers-by and strict specifications for garden sheds and other structures. Even as late as the 1960s, tenants in Oxfordshire were reminded of their good fortune in possessing a garden and of their requirement to look after it. Standards, however, have slipped since then and Ravetz acknowledges the increasing use of gardens for other purposes. Less sympathetically, but no less tellingly, the garden historian Jane Fearnley-Whittingstall claims that 'a perfunctory tour of any council-owned housing estate will reveal that a fairly high proportion of tenants is not interested in using their gardens to grow plants'.[14] She reminds readers of Dylan Thomas's *Under Milk Wood*, in which Polly Garter confesses that 'nothing grows in our garden, only washing. And babies.'

In spite of general trends, in Poundbury the likes of Jane Fearnley-Whittingstall would be pleasantly surprised by much of what she would find. Many of the social housing front gardens are exemplary, as are some of the gardens to the rear. On balance, though, in Poundbury as elsewhere, gardens will not, in the main, be as elaborately developed as those attached to owner-occupied houses; a manifestation of social divisions and differences in levels of disposable income that is actually revealed more starkly rather than obscured by mixing house tenures. It is a potentially emotive subject but, if this can be acknowledged dispassionately, there is at least a chance that these differences can be reduced. For instance, although housing associations are able to install garden sheds, a patio and small lawn, their funding régime currently precludes the provision of certain other facilities that would be of help. A major omission is the inclusion of garages (which would help with storage problems and conceal what might otherwise be left in the open) and, in some cases, even a private driveway. Ideally, they would be able to offer their new tenants (who could have a say in the design, just as owner-occupiers enjoy) a ready landscaped garden; with, say, a couple of fruit trees, some robust shrubs and perhaps even a water feature. It is interesting to recall how gardens were planted for the first occupiers in Bournville. Just as the indoor rooms are fitted with various appliances, there is no reason why the same attention should not be paid by the housing provider to the, no less important, external room. Housing and gardens represent a long-term investment by their providers, and a relatively low level of increased expenditure at the outset could yield valuable social returns.

Rus in Urbe

*'... clean and busy streets within and the open country without, with
a belt of beautiful country and orchard round the walls, so that
from any part of the city perfectly fresh air and sight of far horizon
might be reachable in a few minutes' walk.'* [15]

There is an irony that the above quote, written by John Ruskin and used by
Ebenezer Howard to support his own concept of the garden city, is remarkably
appropriate to describe an aspect of modern-day Poundbury. The irony is not
simply that it was penned against the backcloth of 19th-century conditions,
so much as that the garden cities were designed as relatively low-density
settlements with a more generous allocation of open space than this modern
counterpart. Letchworth and Welwyn, the first garden cities, are altogether
greener places than Poundbury and later versions were to be even more so.
Some of the post-1945 new towns were to take this aspect to extremes,
bringing the countryside in which they were built into the very centre of the
settlement, a true example of *rus in urbe*. Harlow is perhaps the best example
of this, where the master-planner Sir Frederick Gibberd retained as many of
the natural features as possible and used stretches of former countryside to
separate and define his new neighbourhoods.

Poundbury, in its endeavour to remain a compact settlement, is altogether
more economical with greenery within the town than the likes of Harlow. The
street scene relies heavily on the personal efforts of householders to pack their
front gardens with flowers and shrubs, with the addition of communal
planting pockets here and there against courtyard walls. Additionally, along

the main thoroughfares there is a parkway landscape with wide verges sown to grass and lines of young trees. A feature of old Dorchester is its tree-lined roads and splendid town park, and some attempt has been made in Poundbury to replicate the former. It is questionable, however, whether this will be anywhere near as successful. Although the species are carefully chosen and are largely indigenous, the practice of planting them in concrete containers will, as intended, restrict their ultimate growth. The demands of highway engineers and modern health and safety requirements have also limited planting locations; added to which, to the consternation of everyone, one of the building contractors in 2004 felled a long line of semi-mature trees in Poundbury along the western approach to Dorchester. Only in the new squares do the trees really make a significant impact, where the planting of clusters can create an ambience akin to shaded squares in southern France.

There are two organised play areas for children in Poundbury, one within the present phase of development, located at Poundbury Farm amongst the only clump of mature trees, and the other on the southern edge (off Holmead Walk). The urban edge is no more than five minutes or so walking distance from every house, so there is easy access for everyone for informal recreation, with the open countryside beyond. There is also a belvedere (presented by the Prince of Wales to mark the new millennium) with views across to Maiden Castle,

and a little-used surface for the playing of *boules*. Ball yards for older children are planned and other facilities will be added around the edge as Poundbury develops further. These include a new park with a cricket pitch, and a leisure centre with swimming pool (to replace an existing facility in Dorchester).

Another feature that helps to compensate for the small gardens is an attractive area of allotments, or, in Poundbury terms, garden plots. These are sited within the weathered brick walls of the former kitchen garden attached to Middle Farm, and are organised on a voluntary basis through the Poundbury Gardening Society. As well as the usual array of rows of vegetables and flowers, of bean frames and sweet peas, the site enjoys a number of apple

trees planted when this still belonged to the farm. It is an idyllic corner but even this is not without a shadow of uncertainty. With one eye on commercial returns the Duchy has plans to use this land to allow for the expansion of a neighbouring equine surgery. Fortunately for the plot-holders, both the Prince and Leon Krier are keen to see that a replacement site is made available. Moreover, this should be no less attractive than the present one, and there are plans for a new surrounding wall to be built in a traditional cob with tiles along the top, and with fruit trees and quinces along the wall itself. There will be a grassed area with newly planted apple trees and grass paths between the plots, together with benches and a carefully designed tool-house.

This evidence of well-tended garden plots organised communally matches closely the ideal presented in a recent summary of good practice, *Growing in the Community*.[16] The authors, Richard Wiltshire and David Crouch, emphasise the contemporary value of the allotment, not simply for its traditional role in providing a cheap and fresh supply of food but in a wider sense for being so obviously a means of sustainability. Organic vegetables are one thing but allotments are also effective in recycling a host of used materials, ranging from CDs spinning in the wind as a high-tech scarecrow to old carpets laid beneath the surface to conserve moisture and limit weeds. Not least of all, as Poundbury's own garden plots illustrate, allotments encourage neighbourly practices and a lively communal form of organisation. At a time when space for allotments in towns is under increasing pressure, the allocation of an area in Poundbury for its garden plots is a valuable recognition of a need for greenery; their value in this case is increased in relation to the small size of private gardens.

As Poundbury continues to develop there is scope to embrace more fully a commitment to biodiversity, an objective that has only in recent years featured in official planning debates.[17] This welcome national and international initiative to safeguard and enhance the presence of native species, both plant and animal, is applicable within built-up areas as well as in existing stretches of greenery. In the case of the latter, rather than giving everything over to formal parkland it is to be hoped that provision will be made for the retention of pockets of natural chalkland habitat as well, where wild flowers quickly reappear; isolated hedges,

ditches and trees can also play their part. Such pockets would, ideally, be grouped and connected to offer continuous links to the countryside beyond.

Taken together, this outer ring of green space in its various forms amounts to a considerable proportion that will be left unbuilt upon: some 150 acres will remain as open land, compared with 250 acres for the building developments. Poundbury's real garden, though, is the exceptionally beautiful countryside within sight and easy walking distance. Maiden Castle is an obvious focus and a new footpath has been created to improve access from the modern town to the renowned pre-historic site. Beyond that there are numerous other points of interest, and it is not surprising that there is a thriving walking society open to all residents. Tom Johns is the founder of this and tells how it all started after he distributed a flier to the relatively few people living in Poundbury at the time, asking if anyone would like to join him and his wife, Val, on a country walk. Twenty-six people turned up and from there it has gone from strength to strength, with a varied programme of alternating, weekly short and long walks. Tom himself is ideally placed to lead this as, before coming to live in Poundbury, he was an avid walker on his home ground in the Derbyshire hills and a member of a mountain rescue team. He misses the challenging terrain of his former county but, like everyone else, never tires of the exceptional beauty of Dorset's coast and countryside.[18]

Notes

1 Butina-Watson *et al.* (Report, 2004), p.28
2 Brown (1999), p.168
3 Uglow (2004), p.307
4 Jackson (1973), p.149
5 *Ibid.*, p.58
6 Robin Best in the 1950s wrote persuasively about the value of gardens, most notably with R.T. Ward, in *The Garden Controversy*, Wye College, 1956
7 Discussed in Brown (1999), Chapter 5
8 Noel (1999), p.15
9 Quest-Ritson (2003), p.258
10 Butina-Watson *et al.* (Report, 2004), pp.27-28
11 Unfortunately, Daniel Silk has been unable to continue with this enterprising business
12 In Brown (1999), p.157
13 Ravetz (2001), p.118
14 Fearnley-Whittingstall (2002), p.294
15 John Ruskin, in Howard (1898), p.12
16 Wiltshire and Crouch (Report, 2001)
17 For a practical guide on biodiversity, see the Town and Country Planning Association's *Biodiversity by Design* (Report, 2004)
18 Interview with Tom Johns, 17 April 2005

Chapter 6

Growing Community

*'We must consider that we shall be a **a city upon a hill**, the eyes of all people upon us.'*[1]

N ew buildings are one thing; the seeds of a thriving community quite another. The latter is a product not just of good planning but also of an indefinable chemistry. Add to this the fact that in Poundbury the vision is not just for any community but one that was always going to be very much in the public eye and the true measure of the challenge becomes apparent.

Looking to the past, the experience of community-builders is mixed. Pioneering settlements like Bournville and Port Sunlight did well because they offered conditions that were unquestionably better than most of the newcomers had known before, and because there was a conscious attempt to provide far more than simply housing: the place of work was a short walk away and so were places for relaxation and essential needs. Letchworth, the first garden city, grew in fits and starts but was helped by the fact that people only went there because they chose to; as a result, they were more tolerant of early shortcomings and developed a strong pioneering spirit and resistance to the goading of external critics. The experience of planned communities in the mid-20th century was not always so positive, and accounts of that period tell of mixed reactions as some newcomers struggled to get used to a very different type of environment and to manage with minimal facilities in the early stages of development.

Poundbury is still at a relatively early stage of development, but sufficient is in train to give an indication of whether this will evolve into a real community or merely a large housing estate on the edge of Dorchester. Key elements that will determine its future are the extent to which it succeeds in becoming an inclusive social community, the balance achieved between home and workplace, its ability to meet other measures of sustainability, the liveliness of community activities, and its effectiveness in managing itself.

Two Communities or One?

'Poundbury has affordable housing and market housing – and you can't tell the difference between the two. It is a truly mixed community.'[2]

The housing market has never been totally inclusive, and there have always been some who have experienced difficulty in getting a roof over their head. Sometimes this is purely a question of low income, but in other cases there are also health or other social issues involved. For one reason or another, different bodies have intervened over time to provide a safety net for the most needy in society. One of the oldest means of support was the Church, and rows of attractive almshouses in towns and villages that are now much admired often have their origins in this outward sense of religious duty. Especially in the 19th century, housing for the needy was also provided by philanthropists, typically in apartment blocks like the Peabody and Rothschild Buildings in East London and in other cities. It was only towards the end of that century that the State accepted a role in the provision of public housing, initially through local authorities newly charged with powers to build and manage such properties. This latter provision became known as council housing and was a significant feature in the 20th-century urban scene.

Typically, council housing was built in separate developments, away from more exclusive private enclaves, either in groups of apartment blocks or as outer estates of low-rise housing. There was a great deal of innovation and pride attached to this new social experiment, and many of the early schemes were of a higher standard of building and space allocation than in some private housing. Progressive architects were commissioned to work on the apartment blocks and, although the British have traditionally been reluctant to adopt modernist styles, this was one area where such principles were sometimes applied. In the low-rise estates, in contrast, there was a clear preference for a garden suburb layout, and tenants of cottage-style dwellings enjoyed relatively large gardens. Not for many years were council estates to be identified with the very worst of contemporary problems and with an unenviable reputation. Around the country there are all too many estates that bear all of these hallmarks: homes that are not properly maintained, lifts in tower blocks for long out of order, widespread litter and graffiti, burnt-out cars on the streets, a high incidence of crime and rampant drug dealing, and boarded-up shops. It is all a far cry from the hopes and idealism of earlier years.

One response to this worsening situation is an overdue realisation that local authorities are not best placed to manage such massive housing portfolios. The very magnitude of the task, coupled with restrictive work practices, has too often led to situations where councils have become unable to respond effectively if at all to tenant needs. This has been worsened by a lack of adequate funding, combined with inflexible central government controls that limit ways in which it can be spent. As a result, in the latter quarter of the 20th century, all of this led to three important changes: encouragement for tenants to buy the home they were renting; a shift in the role of landlord from local authorities to housing associations; and a move away from the old policy of concentrating all such housing in separate localities. There is evidence of all three trends in Poundbury.

Perhaps the most obvious feature is the last of these, the inclusion of social housing within areas of new development. Initially, in Phase 1, this amounted to about 20 per cent of the total housing stock but in later developments this figure is closer to 35 per cent, or just over one in three of all homes; one proposed scheme in Poundbury (subsequently rejected) even planned to increase this proportion further, to 50 per cent. Moreover, this provision is not geographically concentrated in large groups but is 'pepper potted' throughout the development. It is claimed in publicity for Poundbury and in the sales offices that this housing is indistinguishable from privately owned properties, and visitors like the Deputy Prime Minister who come to see the development for themselves are quick to echo this message. Certainly, the houses are all built to comparable standards and reflect very closely the dominant style of a particular street. One difference, however, is that they are not provided with their own garages (as is done for private houses) and residents have either to

*Examples of
social housing
in Poundbury*

leave their cars in a courtyard or square, or in some cases (where provided) in their own driveway. In just a few instances, sheltered parking spaces (resembling small open barns) have been provided in the courtyards.

A second feature of social housing in Poundbury, also reflecting national trends, is the existence of a housing association as landlord, in this case primarily the Guinness Trust. This is one of the largest housing associations in England, with roots that extend back to the philanthropic actions of the famous brewing family of that name. With a national portfolio of over 25,000 homes, it particularly values its presence in Poundbury, and, significantly, its patron is the Prince of Wales. A second housing association, Magna, has more recently been included in plans for future development, and other housing associations play a specialist role in providing accommodation for the elderly.

The allocation of housing by the Guinness Trust in Poundbury is a transparent process, based on prospective tenants demonstrating an obvious need as well as a strong local connection. From the relevant local authority waiting lists, three nominations are submitted to the Trust for every house on offer, and the family with the highest allocation of points (reflecting greatest need) is offered the tenancy. Emma Coleman is a Trust Housing Officer and tells of a sequence of visits that then follows, first to the successful applicant's present home and then on the day of arrival in Poundbury. Tenants are required to sign both a Trust Tenancy Agreement and the Poundbury Stipulations, the latter applying equally to tenants of social housing and to owner-occupiers. Further visits are made in the event of particular problems that might arise. It is clearly a strength of the system that the Trust applies a very 'hands on' approach in dealing with issues as they arise, and the Poundbury experience compares favourably with that of larger, more traditional estates that the Trust also manages.

Finally, Poundbury is subject, like anywhere else, to nation-wide legislation governing housing tenures and opportunities to buy one's own home, although in the first stages the dominant pattern has been one of housing to rent. This may well change as more houses and apartments come onto the market, with the prospect of a greater variety of schemes on offer, including the Starter Home Initiative, which is aimed to help key workers (particularly health workers, teachers and the police) onto the housing ladder in an area such as this with high property prices.

The mixing of tenures is now a common feature of new housing development in Poundbury, and it is unlikely that further planning permissions would be granted without this continuing commitment. An increase in the proportion to be allocated to social housing since Phase 1 is a reflection of a government commitment to ensure that, nationally, more affordable homes are available and of a willingness by the Duchy to provide them. Whether by expediency or choice, the Prince of Wales himself frequently makes the political point that Poundbury is an inclusive development and that he is in favour of the inclusion of social housing. Duchy representatives have also pointed out that – in spite of serious reservations at the outset by national housebuilders – this tenure mix does not seem to have deterred private buyers. Moreover, in a recent study, the conclusion was drawn that in Poundbury, more than at other locations surveyed, 'tenants and owners talked of living alongside one another politely and happily', albeit without any inclination to mix socially.[3] It would seem on the face of it that this aspect of Poundbury is an unqualified success, although not everyone would necessarily agree.

On the positive side, the quality of social housing is good and, in terms of design and finish, the small groups of houses (usually no more than four) are not in any sense out of place. The point about an absence of garages has already been made, and this does lead to more cars in the open than would otherwise be the case. Rear gardens are no smaller than in neighbouring owner-occupied houses, although, understandably in view of the high costs involved and the lack of storage space, they tend to be less elaborately landscaped than the latter. The real question, though, is not whether social housing looks any different, but whether it works for the tenants, as well as others in the community.

To take, first, the tenants, Emma Coleman points to a high level of satisfaction.[4] She believes that a majority are very positive about living in new housing in Poundbury, and many will see it as an opportunity to make a fresh start. At the same time, it is also accepted that there will always be a minority who really do not fit in and may well not do so anywhere; in such cases the Trust will seek to improve things through negotiation, although in a limited number of cases the situation only resolves itself when the occupants decide to move on. One detects that there are also a few tenants with a sense of outright resentment, like one respondent, a young single mother, who complained that 'you can watch your neighbours polishing their Volvo from your bathroom window. How many single mums and working-class families do you think live here?'[5] On balance, though, 'pepper potting' wins more favour amongst tenants as well as providers than other ways of distributing social housing.

In turn, what is the reaction of private home-owners? It is probably true to suggest that, given a choice, a majority would prefer a development with purely home-owners. There is still a stigma attached to the old idea of council housing, and it is not helped when critics carelessly dismiss Poundbury as just a glorified housing estate. In practice, however, it is unlikely that many 'would-be' buyers have been deterred by the mix of tenures, and the relationship between the two has not proved to be especially problematic. The only instances where this has not been the case are where the Duchy has sought to increase the proportion of social housing in particular sections: there are surely lessons to learn from this experience. On balance, though, Poundbury is a high-density development, and neighbour disputes are just as likely to occur between owners as across the tenure divide. The interests of owner-occupiers are, in any case, at least partly safeguarded by the joint weight of the tenancy agreement and the general stipulations, coupled with responsive management on the part of the Trust. As a last resort (following a legal process culminating in the Courts) tenants may face the ultimate sanction of being asked to leave. For these reasons, while there may well be localised problems, there is probably less chance of repeated nuisance than there would be in an established town.

Fields, Factories and Workshops

'Have your factories and workshops at the gates of your fields and gardens, and work in them.'[6]

Fields, Factories and Workshops was the title of a late 19th-century book by the Russian anarchist Peter Kropotkin, anticipating the dispersal of industry away from the coalfields and into the countryside. Domiciled at the time in England, he rightly saw that the widespread use of electricity would spell the end of overcrowded urban-industrial concentrations and allow a far greater choice of location. For Kropotkin, the anarchist, anything that would lead to the break-up of capitalist strongholds and the formation of more evenly balanced communities was to be welcomed. The anarchist ideal was to look towards a federation of largely self-governing communities, with workshops dotted around the small settlements and with adjoining farmland as a source of fresh food.

Kropotkin had his own political agenda, but the reality is that over the following century aspects of this pattern of dispersal evolved in any case as a natural response to electrification and greater mobility. The advent of personal computers and use of the internet has extended this even further, with a growing number of people able to work at home. Dispersal is now a way of life and there are few restraints on what is possible. This is something that has been recognised in two ways in the development of Poundbury.

First, the very idea of a rural location in Dorset with the ability to attract non-agricultural activities would have been unthinkable before these technological changes. One has only to turn the pages of Thomas Hardy's novels to get a sense of how life was then bound inextricably to the products of the soil and the rhythm of the seasons. The geographical universe of many of his characters was limited if not to the neighbouring village then at least to the nearest market town. All of that has now changed and Dorset is marketed as an ideal place for inward investment, close to the sea and in an area of outstanding natural beauty. Poundbury, with the pull of new housing as well, is, in principle, strongly placed to attract new forms of light industry and office activity.

A second dimension of dispersal has more to do with a relaxation of traditional planning practice which has in the past insisted on a strict separation of home and workplace. In the post-1945 new towns, for instance, it was widely accepted that industry should be located in one or more zones well away from the housing districts. There are still cases where it would not be sensible to locate industry and housing cheek by jowl but, increasingly, there is no reason why the two uses cannot be good neighbours. Additionally, as the new towns have discovered to their cost, locating industry on one side of town and homes on the other is a recipe for traffic problems in peak hours. It is also an essential creed of New Urbanists that a mix of uses is more likely to lead to a lively street scene and the avoidance of areas that are populated only by security guards at night. Additionally, providing jobs locally is an aspect of planning for sustainability, with the aim of locating workplaces within walking distance of homes. For all of these reasons, the Poundbury master-plan made provision from the outset for mixing factories, workshops and offices throughout the town.

More than ten years on, there is reasonable evidence of success on this front, with some 800 jobs in a mix of 40 or so enterprises, ranging from light industry to offices, and advice centres to retail outlets. The Duchy has sought to tread a middle path between meeting its own financial targets while at the same time recognising that some uses would be inappropriate for a tightly-knit settlement. Recognising the need for reassurance by residents that their environment will not be adversely affected by industrial users, and in order to try to stabilise employment opportunities, the Duchy has retained the freehold of such premises and manages the properties through controlled leases.

Industry in Poundbury close to housing

Amongst the industrial users, the largest enterprise is a multi-national firm, Thales, very much at the high-tech end of the spectrum. Another large producer is Dorset Cereals, an expanding

Offices in Poundbury

enterprise that, amongst other things, provides the nation with its breakfast muesli. There is also the nationally known House of Dorchester, 'purveyors of fine chocolates', operating from a purpose-built factory that is popular with residents and visitors alike for its on-site shop. To date, the emphasis has been on industrial users in Poundbury that have given rise to relatively few problems, but a more recent proposal to allocate an area for heavy industry has revealed inevitable local resistance.

Perhaps surprisingly, the demand for office space has not been so buoyant and some of the key sites are occupied by the 'soft' service sector, to include support agencies and advice centres. The Enterprise Centre, for instance, is a corporate training unit operated by Weymouth College; as well as dealing with external organisations it provides networking opportunities specifically for Poundbury businesses. There is also the headquarters of Dorset Cancer Care; and Connexions, an advice centre specialising in the needs of young people. West Dorset is still a difficult market for commercial office developments and the Duchy has had to tread carefully in this early period, offering premises at competitive rent levels in order to attract appropriate users.

Like other new settlements, a retail presence was slow to appear, although this is now changing. A popular arrival in Pummery Square was the Poundbury Village Stores, which is carefully sited to serve the new community as well the adjoining established estate. Other stores of a more specialist nature – a fashion designer and hairdresser, an art gallery and a baby clothes

There is a varied retail presence in Poundbury

shop – front the square. Elsewhere, it is intended that retail outlets will largely be dispersed throughout the town. There will eventually be a town centre for Poundbury – to be known as Queen Mother Square – and this is intended to provide services that will not be in direct competition with established businesses in Dorchester.

In general terms, this policy of mixing uses has not given rise to too many problems. Probably the biggest disappointment for the planners is that, even if people live within Poundbury, there is limited evidence of walking to work. In any case, most of Poundbury's workers still come from outside and the car is the main source of travel, a practice that sometimes gives rise to parking problems on adjoining streets near places of employment. There are also some problems associated with large trucks parking overnight close to one factory in particular, prior to deliveries or collections. In a particular case, a noisy compressor in a factory has been poorly sited and gives rise to a constant nuisance for neighbours. Such problems could be better managed, and it is important to the success of the whole scheme that efforts are made to do so. Poundbury is undoubtedly a more interesting place than a single-use housing estate and, for the benefit of employers as well as the rest of the community, the policy of mixing uses is certainly worth pursuing.

If there is a flaw it lies less in the implementation than in the basic assumption that, given the opportunity, people will choose to work locally. Some already do this – about 8 per cent of residents work in Poundbury firms and another 8 per cent work at home; no doubt more people would choose to live and work locally if sufficient affordable housing were available. There might, however, be quite a low ceiling for these figures; evidence from elsewhere suggests that people will go where job prospects are most attractive. Modern patterns of employment are complex, with one group of employees travelling from home to a different geographical location while passing another group travelling in the reverse direction. Experiments like Poundbury, in seeking to reduce wasteful journeys and improve the quality of life for all, are entirely worthwhile, but one should not exaggerate the likely long-term success of providing a ready source of jobs for local people. Long past are the days when Port Sunlight or Bournville could rely on their employees to walk to work each morning to make soap or chocolate in the nearby, and only, industrial premises.

Living Community

'The reality of human beings is to be found not only (maybe not mainly) in their paid employment ... but also in their engagement in recognised cultural practices.'[7]

Ruth Finnegan's reflective comment above is drawn from her observation of cultural life in Milton Keynes, and, in particular, the vibrant musical scene of amateur choirs and Salvation Army bands, school concerts and Morris Men. Commenting on Finnegan's findings, the anarchist writer Colin Ward takes the view that cultural and other activities flourish in a new community, a result perhaps of a pioneering spirit but often, too, because there are good facilities and access to them is easy.[8] This certainly seems to be the case in Poundbury, where a dedicated core of volunteer residents work tirelessly to support a variety of activities and where the delightful Brownsword Hall serves its community well as a natural focus for regular classes and organised events. This popular community hall, sitting at first floor level on top of its chunky columns, is finely built and carefully finished with the best of natural materials. It was opened in 1999 and management of the building is through the Village Hall Trust, which is responsible not only for operating the hall but also for the upkeep of adjoining Pummery Square.

From time to time, the Square itself is used for events. In June, for instance, it has become customary to hold an evening ceilidh. Everyone in Poundbury is invited, and people arrive carrying picnic tables and chairs, not to mention

The annual ceilidh takes place in Pummery Square

a good supply of refreshments (supplemented by supplies from the Poet Laureate pub, on one side of the Square). A band takes its place in the sheltered enclosure beneath the hall but the dancing is in the open, using the full extent of the Square. The ceilidh is one of the relatively few events that successfully cuts across social boundaries and is popular with children as well.

Social inclusiveness in this regard is not easy to achieve, anywhere, and is not necessarily a sensible goal in the first place; Poundbury is certainly no worse, and probably no better, than other communities of a similar size. We all tend to socialise with those with whom we have most in common, and so long as there are no artificial boundaries to keep people out there is no reason why some activities should not attract more from one group than from another. Some critics seem to enjoy deriding Poundbury as a middle-class enclave but this is to ignore the attraction of a very full menu of activities designed to appeal to residents across the board.

In the regular newsletter distributed by the Residents Association, or through a privately sponsored website,[9] there is a listing of upcoming social and cultural events in Brownsword Hall and Pummery Square. Typically, this listing will include details of yoga classes and 'mums and toddler' sessions, table tennis and karate evenings, and a popular dance studio. Dates are shown for the twice-monthly farmers' market in the Square (a welcome source of income for the Trust) and coffee mornings for various good causes. Poundbury Ladies meet for afternoon talks, and there is a book club and a popular wine appreciation group, the 'Poundbury Wine Knows'. There is also news of a monthly *petit déjeuner* in the nearby Octagon Café, offering French lessons along with coffee and croissants; and that is also the venue for a small but dedicated group of Welsh language speakers. With some distinguished musicians resident in Poundbury a series of concerts is also publicised. Pot luck suppers, quiz nights and auction events for charity make up the regular social calendar, and this is supplemented by seasonal events, such as a summer barbecue and Christmas carol singing.

The arrival in Pummery Square of, first, a coffee shop and, later, a pub added to the opportunities for communal life. The Octagon coffee house is a bright and attractive building that is popular with residents and visitors alike.

Left: Poundbury Ladies enjoy the summer strawberry tea

Below: Farmers' market in Pummery Square

Below right: A popular outdoor sitting area serving both the Octagon Café and the Poet Laureate

Part of the reason is the ebullient personality of its owner, Tom Parsley, who runs it with his wife, Angela. Tom, an émigré from London, moved first to Dorchester, where he was active in local business life before relocating to Poundbury. He is also a member of the Town Council and strongly promotes the fact that Poundbury is good news for Dorchester, with new business opportunities for both. Adjoining the Octagon is Poundbury's pub, the Poet Laureate, originally planned as a hotel but eventually opened as a bar and restaurant with apartments above. Will Hadlow, the pub's first licensee, was at the time of its opening the youngest landlord in England.

One of the ways in which the Residents Association tries to ensure that everyone is aware of what is on offer is through arranging for committee members to visit new householders. This practice follows a long tradition in this country's post-1945 new towns of welcoming new arrivals (often formalised in the past through the work of a social development officer), and in Poundbury this informal arrangement is widely appreciated. These meetings offer an opportunity for newcomers to find out more about the Stipulations that they have signed up to, and to unravel the complexities of the management companies and Duchy responsibilities. There is also a chance to register personal interests in different activities and to find out if these are available locally.

For one reason or another, a very common view is that Poundbury is a remarkably friendly place in which to live. Even though a majority of newcomers will arrive not knowing anyone else in the community, it is not difficult, if one chooses, to become very quickly part of a wide social network.

Research by Oxford Brookes University has borne out what most people know intuitively, that there is a high level of satisfaction with living in Poundbury.[10]

Making Things Work

'The work of building community governance – particularly across tenures – requires all those involved to be willing to undertake a journey to look for the best outcome for the whole community, and to maintain a clarity of vision and purpose.'[11]

Long after the final brick is laid, the enduring record of Poundbury will rest on its ability to safeguard the original concept while at the same time balancing continuing calls for change. This will depend on two things: bringing together the various agencies with an interest in Poundbury's future, and ensuring that the residents themselves are centrally involved in all that happens.

It might be questioned why arrangements should be any different from those in the rest of Dorchester or, for that matter, any other part of Britain. The answer is that Poundbury was conceived and developed as a model settlement, challenging convention at every turn; if normal methods of governance were sufficient to create a place of this sort there would probably not have been a need for the Prince's initiative in the first place. Moreover, there is something self-fulfilling about the process: the very fact that Poundbury was seen from the outset as experimental has attracted residents who are committed to the vision and who are prepared to contribute to its future.

In the early stages there was, understandably, more attention paid to the challenge of building somewhere different and, for the new residents, of simply settling in than to seemingly abstract questions of community governance. The small scale of the early development was also a contributory factor as, with a population of just a few hundred, the 'movers and shakers' were generally known and things could often be settled informally. With the prospect of a fully developed settlement of more than 5000 people the need for more formal structures is already a matter of debate. The task ahead is a little like organising a theatrical production in which the actors are already on stage, jostling for the lead parts; one would not necessarily start from there, but a set of competing interests represents the reality. So who are the key actors?

First, there is the Duchy, currently represented at Poundbury through its own office and a small team energetically led by Simon Conibear, the

Simon Conibear, Development Manager, with his son, Tom (Courtesy: Duchy of Cornwall)

Development Manager. Theirs is an operational role, to secure the realisation of the Prince's vision and Leon Krier's master-plan while at the same time meeting the Duchy's own financial targets. A more strategic role is adopted by Andrew Hamilton, Development Director, who has been involved with the project from the outset and provides an effective link between the operational team, on the one hand, and the Prince and the master-planner on the other. There is also a resident Consultant Architect to call on, in the person of David Oliver.

Importantly, there is no intention for the Duchy to stay on site or in control after the development is complete; by then (except for the industrial premises and a limited number of other properties) the freehold will have passed to individual owners. It is expected, however, that there will be a need for continuing Duchy representation on the various management committees, if only to provide a degree of continuity and links with the original concept of Poundbury.

Next, there is the local authority presence, itself incorporating a hierarchy of different agencies – a county council, district council and town council. With a remit for the whole of the county, Dorset County Council has an important say not only on particular aspects of Poundbury's development but on its very future. In respect to the former, the County is responsible for some of the physical elements, such as the roads and major parts of the social infrastructure (notably, education and social services). As Poundbury continues to grow there will, for example, be increasing pressure to provide additional school places and it is the County that will decide whether to invest there or elsewhere. In the last resort, it is this body that will have a strong say on whether growth in Poundbury will continue to be permitted in preference to other parts of the county that have an equal claim on scarce resources. For electoral purposes, Poundbury is included as part of Dorchester and is represented by two councillors (until very recently just one) for the whole area.

More locally, the responsibilities of West Dorset District Council include the granting of planning consents as well as more operational duties such as refuse collection and street cleaning. It is also the recipient of funding derived from a Section 106 agreement that levies a sum of £5000 from the developers for each home completed, as a contribution towards the cost of additional services. Again, Poundbury is part of a wider electoral constituency, and is currently included in two existing wards, Dorchester West and North. David Barrett is one of the two councillors for the former, and although he lives in Poundbury himself he is adamant that 'Poundbury is part and parcel of Dorchester' and that it should not be seen as a separate entity.[12] He is critical of those who have introduced the term Poundbury Village, as if it were a separate community. In any case, long before the new houses were built, the name Poundbury was in use to denote an adjoining district (to the north of Bridport Road, with historic links to the site of Poundbury Hill Fort) and its wider application has led to some resentment amongst the residents there.

David is an experienced councillor and this is the third area in Dorset where he has held a place simultaneously on both the district and town councils. He is very committed to making Poundbury work and is a champion of better facilities for children and young adults. In spite of this commitment, he sees some potential clouds on the horizon. One is a concern that the necessary services, which would bring benefits to the whole of Dorchester, will be unable to keep pace with the rate of growth. A First School is planned in Poundbury for 2008 but there is now some doubt about its funding because of competing growth plans in the region. He acknowledges the value of the Section 106 levy for each new house but worries that this will not provide enough capital for what has to be done. And, although he is satisfied with the integration of social housing in Phase 1, he believes that the higher proportion required in Phase 2 and after will need to be very carefully managed to avoid future problems.

The third local government agency is Dorchester Town Council, the urban equivalent of a parish council with a range of functions including care for the town's parks and municipal buildings, commenting on planning applications that are dealt with by the District Council, the naming of streets, and town twinning. Councillors are elected and a mayor is appointed to represent the county town as a whole, including Poundbury. Although it is described as a parish authority, there are clearly different interests across the whole of the town and it is questionable whether a single Town Council for all of Dorchester is the long-term answer for Poundbury, with its distinctive character and priorities.

At an even more local level, restricted to Poundbury, there are management companies set up by the Duchy on completion of an area of development to safeguard the future of communal areas. They operate as limited companies, each with its own board of directors (drawn from the particular area it covers), and currently with Duchy representation. At the time of writing there are two of these, Manco 1 and Manco 2, funded through an annual service charge to residents. Mancos have responsibility for areas that have not been adopted by the local authority – for the street lights, trees and shrubs, and for maintenance of the courtyards and road surfaces – and for the communal television system. They are also the ultimate guardians of the Poundbury Stipulations, which specify a 'good neighbours' code.

Peter Noble, Chairman of Manco 2

Peter Noble, the Chairman of Manco 2, believes that the management companies are at a transitional stage and the situation is unlikely to stabilise until the development is complete.[13] Over the next few years he expects that further management companies will be formed, each to represent about 300 homes as well as commercial activities, so that there may be as many as seven separate bodies. By that time, there will be a strong case to amalgamate these into a single company to manage the whole of Poundbury. With an anticipated decline in the Duchy's role, this new 'super Manco' would have prime responsibility for safeguarding the essential principles that have guided Poundbury to date.

Fourthly, there is the Poundbury Residents Association, with a growing membership as new houses come on stream. Peter Bryant is a pioneer member of the community, who with his wife moved to Poundbury in December 1995 and very quickly became involved in local affairs.[14] An earlier attempt to start a Residents Association was foundering and Peter was soon to put his own weight behind the young organisation, becoming its Chairman in 1996 and remaining in that position until 2001. Before coming to Poundbury, Peter had been active in a much larger organisation and so could bring much needed experience to the new body. He recalls that in those early days the key issues were linked to the ongoing building and plans for the future of the settlement, whereas in time this was balanced by more day-to-day concerns. He helped to form good relations not only with the Duchy but also with the local authorities, and it became commonplace for these bodies to include the Association in regular consultations.

Peter Bryant, pioneer member of the community

Mike West, another key community activist who has served as Chairman of the Residents Association

Following the end of his tenure in 2001, there were three successors in as many years (two were to die and one assumed an interim role) before Mike West stepped in to steady the ship.[15] Like Peter Bryant, Mike also brought with him experience of community involvement, in this case from his previous home in south Hampshire. There he had chaired his local parish council and was responsible for a number of valued improvements. His interest in community stems also from a broader context, including membership of various environmental organisations and a longstanding admiration for the Dartington Community, in south Devon.

Mike moved to Poundbury with his wife, Jen, towards the end of 2001, and the two of them very soon threw themselves into community affairs – Jen was drawn into helping with the management of Brownsword Hall and Mike into the Residents Association. Such was Mike's involvement that, following his election in 2003 as Chairman, he has likened his involvement to a full-time job. A familiar sight on the streets of Poundbury is that of Mike cycling with a pack of newsletters to deliver or another meeting to attend. As a former management development specialist with IBM he has well-founded ideas about the value of teamwork and of encouraging individuals to meet their own potential. Gradually, he is helping to re-shape the organisation of the Residents Association to reflect these ideals.

Although all residents, as individual households, are represented through this common association, the Guinness Trust and other housing associations also have a 'say' as major players in the governance of Poundbury.

Additionally, there is an active neighbourhood watch committee, which operates effectively through a devolved network of representatives.

With the prospect of an eventual population much larger than at present, thoughts are turning to a form of organisation that will serve the community well for the future. Through the initiative of the Residents Association, a group has been formed to explore different options. The task is to find a solution that will retain a very local feel for the different neighbourhoods while at the same time offering a means to represent the interests of Poundbury as a whole. District councillors will seek to prevent the exercise becoming, in their eyes, too inward looking and will emphasise the point that Poundbury has to be seen as part of Dorchester.

In the process of looking for a workable solution the participants would do well to take account of the experience of other planned communities. Undoubtedly, the most successful is Letchworth, where the present management body, the Letchworth Garden City Heritage Foundation, has the advantage of a regular flow of income from those of the town's properties that remain in common ownership. The instigator of Letchworth, Ebenezer Howard, had intended that all of the properties would remain so, to ensure that rising property values and additional rental income would be re-invested in the community. Even with partial ownership the Foundation is in the happy position of being able to allocate an annual multi-million pound budget. More than that, the Foundation enjoys a unique set of powers that enables it to respond quickly to development opportunities, without the full paraphernalia of planning procedures. In the words of the Director General of the Foundation, Stuart Kenny, it is really a form of 'benevolent despotism' but with the emphasis very much on 'benevolence'.

Other pioneering model communities, like Port Sunlight and Bournville, have also benefited from benevolent leadership and special arrangements organised through Trusts to safeguard their essential qualities. In contrast, the government-built new towns, for all the idealism that underpinned them, have suffered from their forced transfer to local authority control and at the same time the loss of financial assets generated by their own successful development.

Poundbury is a trend-setter, and it would be unfortunate if its future were to rest solely within a conventional local authority framework. Local authorities are bound by powers and regulations that too often inhibit innovation, and are not necessarily well placed to deal with situations that are somehow a little out of the ordinary. There will undoubtedly be pressures from existing bodies for Poundbury to be integrated into the existing structure for Dorchester but it is to be hoped that a balance can be struck between competing interests. An obvious way forward might be for a single management body to incorporate representatives of the Duchy, management companies, the Residents Association, business interests and local authorities. This management body (which could itself incorporate three or four smaller units to represent the different parts of Poundbury) would be responsible for a defined set of functions related directly to the town's physical fabric; these would include everything to do with street lighting and street furniture, litter clearance, recycling and rubbish disposal, together with local traffic and parking issues. This would ensure that over time there is not a lowering of standards nor the adoption of practices used elsewhere that might not be in the best interests of the model environment.

At the same time, Poundbury is not an island, and it would also make sense to create meaningful ward boundaries for the election of councillors who could play a wider role in Dorchester and the county. There might also be a separately defined Town Council for Poundbury (in addition to the existing one, which should continue to operate for the rest of Dorchester). Moreover, Poundbury is the town that Charles built, and it would be unfortunate if a non-executive place were not also to be found for the Prince's own continuing involvement and ideological commitment.

Notes

1   John Winthrop, speaking to his Pilgrim community as they crossed the Atlantic in the 17th century
2   John Prescott, Deputy Prime Minister, in a speech at The Prince's Foundation's 'Traditional Urbanism' Conference, 20 November 2003
3   Andrews and Smith (Report, 2005), p.18
4   This is further borne out by the findings of Butina-Watson et al. (Report, 2004) in relation to Phase 1 tenants
5   'Fear and loathing in Poundbury', The Independent, 26 August 2004
6   Kropotkin (1899), p.197
7   Ruth Finnegan, in Ward (1993), p.62
8   Ward (1993)
9   http://www.poundburyvillage.com
10 Butina-Watson et al. (Report, 1994)
11 'Community governance for mixed tenure neighbourhoods', summary of research study undertaken by Martin Knox and David Alcock for Joseph Rowntree Foundation, November 1992. http://www.jrf.org.uk
12 View expressed at public meeting at Brownsword Hall, 15 September 2004; also, personal interview, 11 April 2005
13 Interview with Peter Noble, 12 November 2004
14 Interview with Peter Bryant, 19 November 2004
15 Interview with Mike West, 3 April 2005

Chapter 7

Poundbury People

'When the architects have packed their pencils, the diggers clattered off the completed sites, the question that faces the resident as he stands at his front door could be: Does this place feel like home?'[1]

P oundbury is still a new settlement but it is not just the traditional buildings that make it seem as if it has been here much longer. The people themselves who have come to live in Poundbury identify closely with their new place of residence. It feels like an established community.

Some of the new residents have moved only a mile or so from Dorchester, while others have come from further afield; some look back nostalgically to their previous home, whereas others have settled in as if they have been here all of their lives; for some, high-density living has taken a while to get used to, but for others it simply adds to the sense of neighbourliness. Everyone has a view on what is good and what is not, and there are as many viewpoints as people living there. In this chapter, a few of the people of Poundbury speak for themselves.

Roger Parmenter with grandson Ben and Polly

Roger and Jill Parmenter moved with their much-loved dog, Polly, to Poundbury in 2001. They had previously lived for 40 years in the centre of Dorchester, in a rambling Victorian family home. Both ran their own businesses in the town – Roger in electrical retailing and Jill a fashion boutique.

With retirement on the horizon a decision was taken to find somewhere more manageable, a place less demanding of regular maintenance and with a smaller garden. At the same time, it had to be large enough to find room for visiting children and their families, and with extra garage space for Roger's prized vintage Morris car. The outcome was a new three-storey home in Poundbury, designed by the country house architect, Robert Adam.

Roger jokingly describes the move as one to a feudal principality, although he readily acknowledges that if it were not on Duchy land it is unlikely that Poundbury would ever have been built. Overall, Roger and Jill feel that it has been a very good move: they enjoy the quality of their new setting, and are very positive about the opportunities for a lively social life. In spite of living for many years in their previous home in Dorchester, they felt that they would never have got to know well more than two or three of their neighbours, a situation that is dramatically different in Poundbury.

The Parmenters' house is in the same road as the House of Dorchester chocolate factory, but this is not seen as a problem. The factory car park is just large enough to keep employees' cars off the street and the management is sensitive to local needs. Sometimes, articulated lorries turning into the yard disturb the otherwise tranquil street scene, but in general having light industry so close is quite acceptable. Another nearby commercial use, a thriving equine veterinary surgery, is positively welcomed; from time to time, horses are tested for lameness on the street in front of the Parmenters' house, and this a delight to watch.

In contrast, of great concern is the prospect of the planned parkway passing in front of their house, and also a proposal for heavy industry on the other side of the new road, within view of Maiden Castle. Roger has been diligent in collecting articles to inform himself about these issues, and his files bulge with correspondence with the Duchy and other bodies. He invokes the Prince's aspiration to create a place that will enhance the view from Maiden Castle and fears that new factories in this sensitive location would only mar it.

Roger and Jill are enthusiastic supporters of the Poundbury ethos and in different ways cheerfully try to ensure that its best features are safeguarded. An interesting anecdote is that Roger's grandfather, an Essex builder who specialised in churches and missionary halls, was himself involved in a notable experiment in the 1920s to build a model community. In a partnership with F.H. Crittall, he built some of the houses at Silver End, to accommodate workers at Crittall's factory making metal windows. 'I saw a pleasant village of a new order,' said Crittall, 'enjoying the amenities of a town life in a lovely rural setting.' The connection is fascinating and there is more than a little resonance in these words in contemporary Poundbury.

Paul and Debbie Barney, with Josh and Jordan

Paul and Debbie Barney, with their sons, Josh and Jordan, planned to move to Poundbury in July 2003, in time for the new school year. The completion of their new house was delayed for a couple of months, and this meant a period of temporary accommodation in Dorchester so that the boys could start school on time.

The reason for their move from south Hampshire was the consolidation of the House of Dorchester's chocolate production and distribution in Poundbury, where Paul works as Logistics Manager. He bore much of the responsibility for organising the unified operation, including having to train staff in the new systems. Previously he was based at a subsidiary unit in Hampshire, as the factory manager, with a daily commuting journey of more than 60 miles. Now, in the true spirit of Poundbury, he lives and works in the same town, and Debbie also works for the firm. They see themselves as exceptions, as most of the workforce still live in nearby Dorchester or further afield.

Moving with a family to a new part of the world is never an easy task, and especially so when one's roots are in the previous location. Paul and Debbie both grew up in Hampshire and miss having friends and relatives within a short distance. They also left behind an older house, which they feel had more character than a new place, and they also miss the large garden with mature trees. This is all quite a wrench and both recognise that it will take more time to be as settled in their new home. On the positive side, they like the architectural variety of the buildings and appreciate the safety of the streets for their boys.

As is often the case with younger members of the family, the two boys have made the transition with few problems. Because Dorset has a different school system compared with the one they came from, they now attend separate schools; Jordan goes to Damers First School and Josh to Dorchester Middle School. Both will, in due course, progress to the nearby Thomas Hardye Upper School. The rapid growth of Poundbury has more recently put pressure on school places in the locality but Josh and Jordan are a cohort or two ahead of the 'bulge'.

Both boys have made good friends at their new schools and are also active in out-of-school clubs. Josh is a keen Scout, having graduated through the ranks of Beavers and Cubs, and last year spent a week at summer camp along with his younger brother, who is a Cub. Jordan has joined a karate class in Brownsword Hall, and currently has his sights on an orange belt, while Josh has developed a keen interest in hockey. The play areas in Poundbury so far are intended mainly for younger children, and the whole family looks forward to the planned new leisure centre, which will be just a short walk away.

Anna Lewis lives with her partner Neil, her five-year old daughter Holly and their baby son Finley, in picturesque Middlemarsh Street. She moved a few months ago from a smaller house across the road to find extra room for young Finley.

Anna is an exceptional young mother, with her feet firmly on the ground yet with her sights set on new opportunities. She exudes a refreshing sense of happiness and commitment to give her children the best possible start in life. With both Holly and Finley, she decided to stay at home to spend as much time as possible with them in their early years; Holly now attends Damers First School.

By her own admission, Anna is an idealist and enjoys painting and writing poetry; anything to do with Nature captures her imagination. She attributes

Anna Lewis, with Finley and Holly

these interests to time spent doing these things as a child, and to the lasting impression of romantic fairy tales and fantasy novels. Far from squeezing these things out of her life, Anna believes that staying at home with her young children gave her the time and contentment to develop the artistic side of her character. She is pleased to see that Holly seems to have inherited her passion for painting.

Anna comes originally from Dorchester and Neil, a carpenter and joiner, from the nearby village of Puddletown. A couple of years ago, Anna decided that it was time to give some thought to a future career; she knew she did not want to spend her time in an office and looked for something that would, instead, appeal to her artistic instinct. The result was to start a part-time course at Weymouth College that has led to a specialist training in painting and decorating. Next year she will combine college work with an apprenticeship, and after that has hopes of joining Neil and his business partner (together with his wife, herself a painter and decorator) to offer a more comprehensive service.

Although the future is bright, things have not come easily. When Holly was a baby, Anna lived with her in rented accommodation in the centre of Dorchester. She was encouraged to apply to the Guinness Trust for a home in Poundbury, and to her surprise was immediately offered a two-bedroomed cottage. This was the beginning of a new start – from then on 'her whole life has changed' – and she is full of praise for the way that the Trust looks after its tenants. In spite of the perceptions of some of her friends in Dorchester, who believe that Poundbury is a 'snobby' place, Anna finds it very friendly and gets on well with her neighbours. She loves her present house and has bought a stone gargoyle for the porch, replacing a similar one installed by the previous occupier.

In the longer term, Neil and Anna would like to buy a plot of land and build their own house. They are both country-lovers and dream of a place with woods in the background and a stream flowing by. Unlike many dreamers, they have the necessary skills and determination that could bring it all to fruition.

Fiona and Peter Brill

Peter and Fiona Brill tell a story of a lost golf idyll and of discovered new opportunities. Like others who have come to Poundbury, it was the prospect of retirement that triggered a move, in this case from south Hampshire. For 16 years, Peter and Fiona had lived in a dormitory settlement that grew substantially during that period and was destined to continue to do so. They had moved once, from a new house with a small garden to an older property with ample grounds, but once the children had flown the nest it all seemed rather unnecessary and tiresome to maintain. More than that, it was time for a new challenge.

For a couple of years, they visited the many attractive villages in Hampshire and beyond, searching for the ideal place. Thatched roofs and streams running through the main street will always catch the eye, but how easy would it be to make friends and to become part of a community? Poundbury certainly wasn't on their early radar screens, although Fiona had once made a detour to see the place, and they both recalled a television programme featuring the new settlement. That was enough to encourage them to make a visit together. To their surprise, they found a number of new houses under construction, any one of which would have met their needs; they were reluctant to sacrifice internal space but certainly wanted a small garden. An elegant house on one side of a planned square proved the answer and the decision to proceed with its purchase was simple.

If the house was exactly what they wanted, the wider community was at that stage still an unknown quantity. Peter and Fiona moved in during the summer of 2004 and soon after arriving received a 'welcome' call on behalf of the Residents Association. They were told of various activities and, with some trepidation, decided to go along to a forthcoming communal barbecue. As they approached the gathering on open ground on the south side of Poundbury, with Maiden Castle in the background, they were sure that everyone else already knew each other and would have little time for newcomers. Instead, they were warmly embraced and from then on a new web of friends has evolved around them.

Living as the first residents on one side of a square, Peter and Fiona understandably became keenly involved in trying to influence what followed. Their hope was to see the emergence of a landmark square fronted by attractive buildings, with well-planted, communal space. With other residents, they made their views known to the Duchy and were hopeful that at least some of their ideas would be recognised.

On a social front they have found plenty in Poundbury to satisfy their interests. A shared activity is golf, and soon after arriving they both joined the nearest club, on Came Down, high above Dorchester and the coast beyond. Peter, formerly a club captain, wistfully recalls the tranquil parkland course he played on for years, with its colourful rhododendron bushes and carefully tended flowers around the immaculate club house. The hilly, exposed terrain of the new venue, coupled with an occasional sea mist that shrouds the greens, called for changes to their game. In a way, this was the kind of challenge they were looking for when they left their former home, and both have responded well to the different conditions.

With their various priorities now met, they both agree that Poundbury has been a very good move.

Janet Bishop

Janet Bishop is a Poundbury pioneer. She lives in Middlemarsh Street and was one the first occupants, moving into her new house in July 1994 with the painters still at work. Her next-door neighbours took possession at about the same time and, to mark the occasion, were presented with their keys by Prince Charles. Janet recalls that Poundbury was still at that time largely on the drawing board. There was some construction under way, but the land opposite (later occupied by the *Fleur de Lis* retirement apartments) was still open ground. Nearby Pummery Square was not to materialise for another few years.

Before moving to Poundbury, Janet and her family lived in rented accommodation in a village a few miles from Dorchester. It was her husband who read a local newspaper article about this new settlement in the making, and he wrote to the Guinness Trust to see what might become available. The Bishops secured a place on the waiting list and in due course were offered one of the first properties, a two-bedroomed house with its own garden.

Janet now lives on her own in the same house and plans to stay in it; she has already been there for 11 years, longer than in any previous place. Over this period, things have only got better. The days when she lived on a building site are now a distant memory, and she is able to walk just a short distance to the village stores in Pummery Square. She has always liked the fact that Poundbury is planned with everything within walking distance and, as well as her immediate facilities, enjoys what nearby Dorchester has to offer. Amongst other things she is able to visit her daughter there, who lives close to the town centre.

Her neighbours have come and gone and Janet is usually the first to welcome newcomers. She feels that Poundbury offers a good choice of social activities if one wants to participate, but, equally, one can protect one's own privacy. One contribution she makes to community life is to help with coffee mornings in Brownsword Hall. She is also very keen on art and is thinking of trying her own hand in a class. Retirement offers more opportunities than when she went out to work each day and this is one interest she would like to explore.

Janet is full of praise for her landlord, the Guinness Trust, and cites instances of its prompt and efficient response when maintenance issues arise. With the Trust's approval, she has been able to make changes to both the interior of her house and to her garden to meet her own needs. She likes the practice in Poundbury of mixing tenures and gets on well with her neighbours.

The story of Janet and her family is a striking illustration of the continuing role of the Guinness Trust. At the time that Poundbury was started, in a depressed housing market, private developers were wary of making the first move; were it not for this early commitment to social housing, the building of Phase 1 would almost certainly have been a slower process.

Angus and Ann McIntyre recall Valentine's Day 2003 with special affection. Living in north Cheshire at the time, they spent the weekend in the tranquil Devon resort of Sidmouth, with plans to visit nearby towns and villages in an ongoing quest for a new home. They had made earlier visits to Devon to no avail and, enjoyable as it was as a weekend break, this visit looked like being no more successful. On the Monday morning they left Sidmouth, travelling eastwards to see Angus's mother in Southampton before heading back to

Ann and Angus McIntyre

Cheshire. A short detour along the way was to change everything.

Dorchester is sited just north of the A35, and drivers on the bypass get a glimpse of Poundbury in the making. That was not enough in itself to entice them to see more and they continued on their way into central Dorchester. At the suggestion of estate agents in the town, and their own growing curiosity, they looped back to Poundbury, which was then in its tenth year. They liked what they saw and decided there and then to put down a deposit on a new house; they had only left the A35 to buy a sandwich for lunch but ended up making the most expensive purchase of their lives!

Angus and Ann had clear criteria for where to live: it had to be somewhere with a pub, a general store that sells newspapers, a golf course nearby, accessible health facilities and good shops within reach. Being close to the sea would be an added bonus. Poundbury could meet all of these requirements and more. Originally, they had hoped to find these things in a well established village, but the reality of contemporary villages is that they have few facilities of their own and create a culture of car dependency.

Just 12 weeks later the McIntyres moved in. They had lived in their previous family home, in a dormitory village near Warrington, for 26 years and came to a place where they knew no-one. If it was a bit of a gamble it became apparent almost from day one that it would pay off. Angus and Ann are a naturally sociable couple and had little difficulty in making new friends and very quickly getting involved in community life; more than that, they have themselves contributed actively to the organisation of a number of activities. Ann joined and helped to organise Poundbury Ladies, took part in a weekly 'Keep Fit' class, and also helped with events in Brownsword Hall; Angus became an active member of the Poundbury Investment Club, and in the following year a Director of one of Poundbury's management companies. Together, they participate in many of the mainstays of community life – centred around Pummery Square – from the wine appreciation group to regular quiz evenings, and from pot luck suppers to celebration events in the

Poet Laureate. Their adult son and daughter are delighted to see them happy in their move.

An interesting footnote is that, as a professional civil engineer, Angus's job had taken them, first, to Milton Keynes in its infancy and then to Warrington. Both were new towns, and they are now able to bring this joint experience of planned settlements to support the growth of another new community.

Paul and Clare Newman, with Jessica

Paul and Clare Newman are now living in their third house in Poundbury and, uniquely, represent one of four generations of their family living in the new settlement.[2]

Their own story started when they were married nine years ago and chose to live in a new house, not least of all to avoid the chores of DIY. Both had grown up locally and Poundbury was an attractive location; Paul's parents were already living there and had been one of the first households, living at the time in Holmead Walk. Even as recently as the mid-1990s it was possible to secure a new property with a £50 deposit, and Paul and Clare alighted on a terraced cottage in Brookhouse Street for their first home. From there they soon moved on to a larger house in nearby Hintock Street, and then to their present home, a grand, detached Georgian-style villa on Peverell Avenue East. Paul's parents have also moved from their original home but still live just a short walk away, and his grandmother moved from a nearby village to another house in Poundbury, which she shares with her sister. To add to the family network, Clare's parents live barely a mile away in the old district of Poundbury, in west Dorchester.

Paul and Clare have two daughters, Jessica and Bethany, and feel that the house and its setting offer all that they need. Jessica currently attends a First School, built just six years ago, not in Poundbury itself but within walking distance. She has friends from her school in some of the houses nearby, and enjoys being taken to the recently opened Middle Farm play area. When Jessica was younger, Clare joined another young mother to start a 'mother and toddler' group in Brownsword Hall and, although she no longer organises it, is pleased to see it continuing to thrive. For a short period, Clare worked in the then newly opened village stores, and enjoyed meeting her friends and others who came into the shop; as well as meeting local needs, the shop has become an important focus of community life.

Four generations of the same family in Poundbury is an obvious source of interest and it is not surprising that the Newmans were invited to meet Prince Charles on one of his regular visits. They were also introduced to the celebrity television doctor, Dr Hilary Jones, when he opened the Castle View nursing home.

Although most of their family life centres on Poundbury and its environs, Paul travels by car to work in Poole, where he is a specialist engineer making components for aircraft. Poundbury has been planned to offer local employment opportunities, but Paul's experience is a good illustration of the impossibility of meeting everyone's specialist needs. Reducing the number of car-borne journeys to work remains a laudable goal but the idea of achieving a perfect match between home and work is no longer realistic in modern society.

Sue McCarthy-Moore is one of still relatively few who live as well as work in Poundbury. More than that, she runs her own business and has done so for ten years.

Sue trades under the name of Stitchinghouse Design and occupies a shop and workplace in a prominent location in Pummery Square. She specialises in soft furnishings and interior design, and also makes specialist clothing; the

Sue McCarthy-Moore, with her daughters and pet dog

elaborate costume of the Dorchester Town Crier is a prime example of her inventiveness. If a wealthy celebrity were to ask for 'out of the ordinary' wedding gear she would undoubtedly relish the challenge.

Before coming to Poundbury, Sue worked from her then home in Dorchester. She liked the idea of the new community because she could see the possibility of renting a purpose-built workshop, ideally in a cluster with others, without having to resort to the soul-destroying environment of an industrial estate. In fact, Pummery Square is her fourth location and she has had to show resilience along the way. Her first premises were in what is now the veterinary surgery in the Middle Farm buildings; then, on a temporary basis, she relocated to an unoccupied house; before moving again, this time to Burraton Yard, with hopes (unfulfilled, as it transpired) that other craft units would follow. The failure of Burraton Yard to evolve into a thriving crafts centre is one of Poundbury's missed opportunities, although it would still be possible to include such a scheme in a later phase of development.

The present location of Stitchinghouse in Pummery Square is proving a good move, and her business got the Royal seal of approval with the Prince of Wales officially opening the shop; the Duchess of Cornwall has also paid a visit. Because of its prominent position, the shop attracts visitors as well as local residents and many of her clients come from outside the town. After ten years in Poundbury, Sue's work has an excellent reputation and much of her new business is a product of personal recommendation.

Another attraction in moving from Dorchester was the prospect of living as well as working in the same community. For most of her time in Poundbury, Sue lived in a rented house in Middlemarsh Street, where she was one of the first residents. A familiar landmark on the street was the stone gargoyle in her porch, which her daughters named 'Gizmo'; when she moved from that address the new tenants replaced it with a similar cast. Another street feature is Sue's treasured, blue MGB Roadster, affectionately known as 'Albert'.

Early in 2005, Sue bought a new house in Phase 2 and is still busy getting it into shape. Especially because she works locally she regards her house as something of a retreat, a place to relax in after a day in the thick of it. To help with this, she has designed a very attractive water feature for her garden, with channels at different levels. When deciding on her new home, Sue had no doubts about staying in Poundbury. She has made many friends over the years and enjoys the varied architecture. If she could make one change, it would be to add to the prevailing traditional styles a few examples of the best of modern architecture. This is surely an idea worth considering.

Isobel Hallett, with her dog, Marcus

Isobel Hallett is a remarkable lady and, at the age of 94, Poundbury's oldest resident living independently. With her dog, Marcus, a Yorkshire terrier, she moved to Poundbury in September 1999.[3] Before that she had lived with her husband in a large bungalow in nearby Broadwey, near Weymouth. After her husband died, in 1998, Isobel decided that it was time to move to somewhere more compact, and with a daughter already living in old Poundbury, in west Dorchester, she took the decision to move to her present home.

Isobel recalls that when she arrived there were few houses around and to start with it was really quite lonely. Then, one day, a neighbour invited her to coffee, where she met some other ladies, and from there the informal meetings evolved into the popular Poundbury Ladies group. Like everyone else, her view is that this is the most sociable place she has lived in, and she soon got to know a wide circle of friends. Every morning she takes her dog for a walk and invariably meets someone along the way. She jokingly says that she is known either as 'the little old lady with a dog' or 'the lady with a little old dog'. If there is one minor drawback to her location it is that her neighbours on either side use their houses as second homes.

Poundbury suits Isobel well. She loves her house and is planning to add a conservatory to give her more space. The arrival of a general store and hairdresser in Pummery Square were welcome events, and she makes use of the nearby Octagon Café for lunch. There are fund-raising coffee mornings in Brownsword Hall that she attends, and she looks forward each year to the summer evening ceilidh in the square. She is well-known and much liked for her kindness; one friend who dropped in during this interview described her as '200 per cent gold'.

On her 90th birthday, Isobel left her garden gate open so that friends could drop in for a drink and something to eat. As well as people she knew, four visitors to Poundbury, who were simply looking around at the time, were invited to join the gathering; since then she has exchanged Christmas cards and kept in touch. There was food left over after the party and she called down some workmen from the scaffolding of a nearby building to take it away with them. The workmen befriended her and were sorry when they later had to move to another part of Poundbury.

A memorable occasion was when Prince Charles, on one of his regular tours of Poundbury, paid her a visit; as the oldest person living on her own, the Prince asked if he could come and see her. 'I didn't curtsey,' she said, 'or I might have fallen over!' She recalls that she had a rice pudding in the oven when he arrived and that the Prince remarked on how delicious it smelt. To her surprise he asked to see the rooms upstairs and Isobel was thankful that she had cleaned them well before. Her only regret is that, in the excitement, she forgot to offer him a cup of tea!

Gordon and Jane Ashdown are the ultimate New Urbanist couple, dividing their time more or less equally between the two leading trans-Atlantic experiments, Poundbury and Seaside. Their story goes back even before this episode, to the early 1970s, when they moved to the site of an earlier attempt to break the mould of urban development, New Ash Green in Kent.

Gordon is an architect and Jane a teacher, and for some 15 years, when Gordon worked as Chief Architect for the oil conglomerate Exxon/Mobil, they lived with their young family in Toronto. Like others in the North American snow belt, the prospect of a winter vacation in the sun was always enticing and their present episode really dates back to a Christmas break at the end of 1990. Following a stay in the Florida Keys they decided to drive north and take in a relatively unknown stretch of coastline in the north-west of the State, known as the Florida Panhandle. As they drove along the shoreline, with the emerald waters of the Gulf of Mexico on one side of the highway, their

Gordon and Jane Ashdown

reactions were mixed. Although it was not at that time heavily developed, there were already signs of the kind of characterless sprawl and tasteless commercialisation that was more in evidence further south. They drove through Panama City Beach, the epitome of all that was wrong with brash modern development, and shortly afterwards came across a place that, although in its infancy, was growing in a totally different way. The place they discovered was Seaside; the time New Year's Eve.

So began a love affair with this New Urbanist resort settlement that has grown in strength over the years. Each year after that they made the marathon 1200-mile journey from Toronto, driving in turns for 20 hours until at last they could see the original water tower rising above the surrounding tree-line. Seaside was, in the early 1990s, still at an early stage of development, but there were already houses to rent and new experiences to share with annual vacationers like themselves and the small core of owners who lived there permanently.

In due course, they were able to buy their own apartment in neighbouring Seagrove and to continue to be part of the Seaside community. The development of Seaside and their own lives became increasingly inter-twined. It seemed perfectly natural when their daughter, Polly, chose to be married on a beach setting in Seaside, and later when Gordon and Jane favoured their adopted home to celebrate with their extended family their own 40th wedding anniversary.

While still in Toronto, they kept their links with England, returning every couple of years for visits to relatives and to some of their favourite haunts. Dorset was always included in this itinerary and, at about the same time as they discovered Seaside, Gordon read about the Duchy's plans for Poundbury. They visited the exhibition that was held in a shop in Dorchester's High West Street and watched the building of the first houses. When, in 1999, they left Toronto they decided to make Poundbury their new home, moving first to a small cottage and in the following year to a larger place (called, after a much-loved family cat, Blanco's Cottage). The rest is history, with most of the winter months spent in Seaside and the rest of the year in Poundbury.

Notes

1   *Poundbury 10th Anniversary Exhibition Review* (2003). Produced in association with *Dorset Magazine*. Poundbury: Poundbury Publishing

2   Since this interview Paul and Clare have moved with their family to their fourth house in Poundbury, in Woodlands Crescent

3   Sadly, since this interview Isobel's dog, Marcus, has died

Chapter 8

Seaside Excursion

'Seaside, a small community in Florida, is almost always held up as an exemplar of New Urbanist design principles.'[1]

Poundbury is the first fully-fledged New Urbanist experiment in Britain but not the first internationally. Seaside in Florida, USA, pre-dates Poundbury by more than a decade and, for all its differences, is frequently acknowledged as an influential source of ideas and a demonstration that a place that so obviously flouts convention really can work. For these reasons, this chapter records the findings of a trans-Atlantic excursion to compare experience.

Beside the Seaside

'I find it delightful to sit under a ceiling fan on a hot afternoon and just talk to passing neighbours.'[2]

Seaside is located in the Florida Panhandle, the north-western extension of the State fronting the Gulf of Mexico that belongs more to the American South than the rest of the 'Sunshine State'. It is an easy place to find, contrasting

Robert Davis was keen to create a traditional, 'folksy' environment where people could feel at home

favourably in appearance with the nondescript and ramshackle development that sprawls elsewhere along much of this flat coastline. Nearby Panama City to the east of Seaside – the centre of what was once disparagingly known as 'the Redneck Riviera' – is the region's Blackpool or Benidorm, a holiday mecca of motels and high-rise condominiums for blue-collar workers and their families from the prospering commercial cities and industries of the South. Westwards along the coast to Pensacola there are similarly depressing scenes of brash beach-side development.

Seaside itself is not a large settlement but its influence has been disproportionate, attracting a constant stream of visitors and influencing architects and planners not only in America but internationally too. When the Prince of Wales wrote *A Vision of Britain* in 1989, Seaside was already sufficiently advanced to be cited as 'an extraordinary place'. Like Poundbury, it took a wealthy sponsor to conceive and back the experiment, although in this case not a prince but an exceptional property developer, Robert Davis. For Davis, this was always going to be more than a mere real estate venture and from the outset he wanted to create a traditional, 'folksy' environment where people could feel at home. But he also had more than an eye for sustainability: 'The idea of a neo-classical town is that it has pedestrian scale which obviously gets people out of their automobiles and uses up a great deal less petroleum. In addition to that there are limits to a town like this – it should have boundaries or edges beyond which there should be open space.'[3]

Davis is widely admired for his idealism and for being prepared to match his ideas with financial backing, and professionals readily acknowledge his personal influence on the project: 'Davis among developers is remarkable. He is marked by idealism and moved by idealism. He has devoted his life to the creation of a modern American utopia, at least within the framework offered by contemporary American society and the current-day ideas of the flow of property and money.'[4] The fact that Seaside has also proved to be a great commercial success has undoubtedly led to it being taken more seriously than it would otherwise have been.

It was, in fact, Davis's grandfather, J.S. Smolian, who with great foresight purchased the 80-acre site as long ago as 1946.[5] Each summer, grandfather Smolian, a department store owner from Birmingham, Alabama, would come with his family to spend their summer vacation on the Gulf coast. When he bought the land – dismissed at the time as worthless sand and scrub – he had thoughts of turning it into a summer camp for his employees, to be known as Dreamland Heights. Nothing came of these plans and on his death in 1978 the estate was passed to his grandson, Robert. In the event, Robert inherited not only the land but also his grandfather's vision of transforming it into a place to cherish. At the time of the bequest, with an educational background in history and later at the Harvard Business School, he had already gained experience in real estate development. It was that experience, combined with fond memories of childhood vacations along this warm and enticing coastline, which encouraged the ideas that eventually became Seaside.

An early attempt to capture the traditional domestic architecture of the South

At the heart of Davis's vision was the idea of replicating the kind of building that once typified this stretch of the South. He recalled time spent on annual holidays in attractive wood-frame cottages with generous porches shaded by deep roof overhangs, and with gentle breezes blowing beneath the raised floors and through the well-ventilated rooms. The details of good housing, well adapted to local conditions, had been worked through over successive generations of home-owners and he knew

Traditional features are an integral part of the architecture, and colours are generally taken from a limited palette of pastels

that it was the secrets of that experience that held the key to future success. With his wife, Daryl, he made extensive trips through the region – not only in north Florida but also in neighbouring Georgia and Alabama – to observe and document the intricate details of vernacular architecture and small-town design that would, in due course, provide the building blocks for his own development.

As well as learning from what he saw, Davis was also widely read and in this formative period acknowledged the influence on his own thinking of the works of Leon Krier. One of Krier's beliefs that caught his imagination was the importance of developing parcels of land of the right size. Krier had actually singled out the attraction of 80 acres as an ideal unit of development – equivalent to a quarter-mile radius – as this amounted to the distance that a person would comfortably walk on a daily basis to go to work, to shop, or to a café or restaurant. One might have to use a car to go to a concert or a ball game, but there should be no need to do so just to buy a quart of milk or to take your children to school. Taking his cue from Krier, Davis decided that his holding was ideally placed to develop into a well-balanced little township, characterised by traditional forms of architecture and recovering a lost sense of civic intimacy.

Perhaps Davis's most telling decision was to commission Andres Duany and Elizabeth Plater-Zyberk, then relatively unproven architect-planners with innovative ideas, to help him take forward his plans. Davis was not impressed with the first designs, recognising that the buildings would look vernacular but were, in fact, modernist in detailing with alien features like sliding-glass doors. There was more work to be done and, like Davis had done before, the architects realised that authenticity could only be found in the hidden by-ways and sleepy small towns of the Southern countryside. It was not before they could make their own detailed field studies that agreement could be reached on the essential detailing for the new development.

It was in the planning of Seaside that Duany and Plater-Zyberk prepared the first of their pattern books, 'a system of codes prescribing in considerable detail the placing of buildings, setbacks, lot lines, fences, road widths, style even, window design and so forth'.[6] Every house in Seaside had to have a porch, and all the picket fences were to be made of real wood and painted white. Nor was it just the initial design that was prescribed; owners were also given a limited choice of colours from which to paint their houses. At the same time, there was plenty of scope for individuals to introduce interesting features such as towers, pavilions, follies and gazebos. 'They believe that with the Code anyone can design his own house here – you don't have to be an architect.'[7]

Breaking with tradition, Duany and Plater-Zyberk refrained from taking commissions for the design of individual buildings. They put their faith, instead, in the versatility of their codes, which they believed could be applied effectively by builders as well as professional architects. Depending on the location of a particular plot of land, the building code specified one of eight house types, ranging from single-storey traditional homesteads to up-market ante-bellum mansions. Although there is a formal approval process for individual designs, with the Town Architect as final arbiter, the approach has been refreshingly pragmatic – intentionally so, to encourage diversity within defined parameters.

It was always intended that there would be more to Seaside, however, than a mere collection of buildings, no matter how well designed, and to ensure that it would become a true township Davis turned in 1980 to his previous mentor, Leon Krier, to assist in refining the master-plan. The brief was to provide a plan that would encourage everyone to walk for life's daily requirements and to foster a sense of civic life. Davis wanted 'an environment that would draw people out of their houses and onto their porches' and 'an atmosphere of neighbourliness'. It was a conscious attempt to address the neglect of public space that has been the bane of modern urban planning in the United States. Small towns had not traditionally turned their back on the public domain and Davis was determined at Seaside to re-assert its importance. Instead of a fee for his work, Krier accepted a building plot where he would later design his own house.

Pastel Coloured Utopia

'I remember spending the day walking around and I fell in love with this place ... it had an unusual surrealist feel about it, like pastels run amok.'[8]

To mark their confidence in the project, Robert and Daryl moved in 1980 to one of two pioneer homes in Seaside, ahead of the completion of either the master-plan or the building code. Known as the 'Yellow House' it was designed by Davis himself, as was the neighbouring 'Red House' that was for a time used as Seaside's estate office. The simplicity of these single-storey structures, compared with the exotic character of later buildings, reflects the impact of subsequent rising land values. At the outset, Seaside was seen by real estate onlookers as a wayward experiment that would never succeed in commercial terms. Davis thought differently and, helped by low land values in its pioneering days, it seemed entirely appropriate to set one's sights on the kind of modest homestead that in the back country where it originated would often have been seen as little more than a shack. In fact, the folksiness of it all very soon attracted its own premium value and land prices rose sharply to a situation where in 2005 individual plots facing the sea would sell for a million dollars or more. Buyers in this new market were no longer going to be satisfied with a shack with a tin roof and, while still working within the codes, later structures have made far more intensive use of the land.

In some ways, Leon Krier set the pace for a new style of seaside mansion, building high on a small plot and including what has now become the kind

Robert and Daryl Davis's 'Yellow House' was intended to set the tone for what followed

'Krier Cottage', repainted by the present owners

of tower that is characteristic of Seaside. Strangely, in spite of his earlier reputation and the widespread influence of his ideas, Krier had not previously undertaken a practical architectural assignment. Seaside offered the challenge he had been waiting for: 'I always said I would never build unless the conditions were right; Seaside was a dream come true.'[9] Modestly named 'Krier Cottage', it is, in fact, an imposing building, modelled on Greek revivalist principles, although deceptively with only one room per floor and just one bedroom in the house. Particularly as it is on the highest point in Seaside, from the outside the most prominent feature is the studio/temple tower on the top floor; from the inside this enjoys striking views of the sea and the surrounding landscape.

Towers have become an iconic feature of Seaside, extending the number of houses with sea views. To accord with the building code these have to be slim

Towers, in various shapes and sizes, are now an iconic feature of Seaside

Quirkiness is a feature of Seaside

structures to avoid blocking the views of others, and across the town one can see their users gathering with a glass in hand for the evening sunset. Duany is enthusiastic about their impact: 'it seems that Seaside is going to be a city of towers, unlike any other I know of in America'.[10]

Not that towers are the only iconic feature: picket fences, porches, roofs and windows are all part of the same story, and building materials used are, as far as possible, of natural products that age well. Picket fences are an interesting feature, a bit like the ubiquitous chimneys in Poundbury, conveying an immediate sense of old-world charm. Although all are painted white, no one design in a street is the same as another, leading to an inventive variety of motifs. As well as typifying the vernacular theme, the low fences also perform a practical function in defining a sense of edge while encouraging the idea of walking past neighbours' homes and calling across to owners sitting in their porches. Enthusiasts see these fences as a vital contribution to a real sense of community: 'as they have done for centuries throughout the world, Seaside's picket fences invite meandering, encourage neighbourliness and conversation, and gracefully announce the presence of genuine civic life'.[11]

Every house in Seaside is required to have its own front porch, and most of these are well used, with attractive rockers and coffee tables permanently in place. They are seen as a transitional area between the public realm and private space, where neighbours can share a sense of belonging to the same community. It is not uncommon for houses to have side and rear porches as well, not simply for effect but as a well-tried method of dealing with the high summer temperatures and humidity.

Roofs are another distinctive feature and the building code is specific about rooflines and materials to correspond with what is typical of the region. An interesting issue arose when some of the early owners chose to use tin for

A typical 'Krierpath' with sandy surface and vegetation

Beach pavilions are a feature much loved by the residents and visitors alike

their roof-covering and other residents objected fiercely, complaining in barely veiled racist terms that Seaside would soon resemble 'Tobacco Road'. In spite of that, later buildings have in some cases continued to use tin. Windows are another defining feature, closely specified in the building code. The aim is to be consistent with Southern traditions of vertical and square windows, sub-divided with wooden frames, as opposed to the use of large undivided picture windows that has become the norm in speculative housing estates.

Walking or cycling through the streets and across the squares of Seaside, the scene is one of constant interest and delight. Behind the white picket fences, houses are painted from a rich palette of pastels and in a few cases (generally set back towards the rear of the settlement) more strident colours. The natural vegetation has matured over the years and the gardens (larger than Poundbury's but still quite close-knit) display a variety of indigenous shrubs and trees: oaks and magnolia, rosemary and sea oats. In fact, the architectural code precludes the planting of anything that is not indigenous, and lawns (which would require sprinkling and a wasteful use of water) are forbidden. Narrow sandy paths wind their way between the plots, a feature highly unusual in American towns and known locally as 'Krierpaths' in recognition of their source of inspiration.

Name boards tell an interesting story of provenance and aspirations

This is a resort community but even as more people settle permanently it is the sea that draws people here, and this is reflected in the ease of access to the waterfront. A striking feature is that of the beach pavilions at the end of the north-south roads, each designed differently and offering a natural point of gathering for its nearest residents, as well as a focal point on the skyline. Beyond the pavilions are the famous boardwalks that take users safely across the vulnerable dunes onto the white sands beyond. This is undoubtedly a place to enjoy and every morning one can see groups of walkers and joggers making their way along the shoreline, breathing in the tangy Gulf air and acknowledging that life does not really get any better.

There is also a real sense of fun and pride about the place, exemplified in the folksy name plates attached to the picket fences for each house. Printed informally in blue against a white background, each tells its own story of who owns the house and where they come from. The names of these largely holiday homes are also evocative. Bob and Marie Alcorn hail from Knoxville, Tennessee, and have named their seaside arcadia 'Art and Soul'; Sean and Erwin come from Alpharetta, Georgia and live in 'Homecoming'; while Henry and Golda Levy, from upstate New York, must surely take the prize for nomenclature with 'Seduction by Water'. Elsewhere, one passes 'Bunny Hop' and 'It's Always Five O'Clock', 'Heavenly Scent' and 'Somewhere in Time', 'Life is Good' and 'As Good as it Gets'. Measured in terms of resident satisfaction, the last of these house names, 'as good as it gets', might well be applied to the town as a whole. In fact, in some early publicity literature Seaside was described as 'the little beach town that made a big difference by remembering how nice the world can be'.[12]

Although it's easy to be distracted by the undoubted appeal of the architecture, the prime movers in its formation would probably prefer Seaside to be defined by the contribution of its public space. For this was always intended to re-create something of the sense of community and collective experience that was taken for granted in traditional American towns, in the days before downtown activities were abandoned in favour of a suburban mall culture. Small though it is, Seaside would buck current trends with its post office and general stores, its own church and school, and all within walking distance of every home. People talk of the 'Popsicle factor' to describe the ability of a child to hop on a bike and cycle safely to the local store for an iced lolly.

A popular venue for that kind of errand is Modica Market, founded by Charles and Sarah Modica, and offering an intriguing mix of everyday goods and exotic deli products. The store offers a delivery service, using an old-fashioned bicycle with an iron-frame basket attached to the front. Daryl Davis was instrumental in helping to get this and other stores started, seeing them as an essential component of early community life. Before the first shops materialised she took the initiative in introducing a Saturday market close to the highway, and personally brought in produce from local farms and bakeries. There is now a healthy variety of businesses in Seaside, including a good bookshop, a cycle hire firm, a shop that sells only goods with a Seaside motif, and an open-air fashion market called Perspicacity; not to mention the ice cream parlours and sushi bar, Roly Poly's deli sandwiches and the local oyster stall. And every evening as the sun sets a 300-pound bell is rung from the top of a tall, weather-boarded tower, marking the end of another day and time to enjoy a 'sundowner'. A popular venue for this is on the balcony of Bud and Alley's, a first-floor bar and restaurant overlooking the beach.

Not by bread alone, the making of a community is dependent on more than the mere building of shops and houses, no matter how good they might be, and a constant aim has been to make room for a thriving artistic life. Ruskin Place, just off the main square, is where artists have been encouraged to make and sell their products. Paintings, sculptures and Southern antiques line the European-style pavements. A repertory theatre company has been

The open-air boutique, Perspicacity, and an ice cream parlour are typical of Seaside's shops

A real attempt has been made to attract artistic ventures

formed and the amphitheatre in the centre of the downtown area is a natural setting for performances. To support the arts a 1 per cent levy is added to every purchase in the town.

As in any new settlement, there is always a potential bridge to be crossed in providing a full range of facilities prior to reaching a sufficient threshold population to fully support them. The problem is exacerbated at Seaside as there is only a minority at any one time – certainly no more than 30 per cent – who live there permanently, although the actual population is higher than that as a result of holiday lettings. In spite of this, a fair balance has been struck, with most of the services now in place, the main exception being to complete the downtown ring of buildings around the central amphitheatre. Critics have pointed to the isolation of two arcaded terraces of shops and apartments at either end of the central crescent, although there are now firm plans to fill the gaps. When that is done it will be time enough to take a measured view of what has been achieved, particularly in the innovative use of public space.

Keller Easterling, who made a detailed study of Seaside at the end of its first ten years, wrote even then that the 'town's chief innovation has less to do with its buildings and more to do with the space between the buildings and the buildings' response to space'.[13] She affirms that it is a rediscovery of small-town urbanism that has informed the plan and sees the essential challenge as being to create a place that can somehow balance common themes with the unexpected: 'the magic of the small town lies in its potential to create urban jazz – to allow for anarchy and variation within a rhythm and tune'.[14] Seaside plays its own version of urban jazz, mellowed by the background notes of the sparkling surf rolling onto white sandy beaches.

Celebrating Seaside

*'I believe that the lessons they're working out in Seaside have very
serious applications, both in rural areas and in our cities.'*[15]

Before he embarked on the Poundbury project, the Prince of Wales (as the
above quote illustrates) had already singled out Seaside as breaking new
ground and offering inspiration for others. This is how things so often work:
it is always easier to promote ideas when there is already a practical exemplar.
Time and again, Seaside would be held up as a shining example of a new
approach to urbanism, just as Poundbury itself would later be used in this way.

The fact is that Robert Davis bucked a trend in the United States – of
characterless suburban development that had been driven relentlessly by the
conservatism and undiluted profit motive of real estate developers,
particularly since the 1940s – that seemed to lesser mortals irresistible. Fired by
a belief that things could be done better he brought into play not only his own
outstanding business acumen but also an ability to pick the right team. Andres
Duany, Elizabeth Plater-Zyberk and Leon Krier, although all relatively
unproven at the time, emerged as stars in their own right and Davis was wise
enough to give them sufficient creative space. The outcome is that for a tiny
settlement extending over just 80 acres the impact of Seaside has been
disproportionate. There is evidence of this both locally and across a wider
realm of influence.

Whether travelling to Seaside from west or east along the two-lane coastal
Highway 30A one can see striking examples of later projects based on
comparable principles. Developers and bankers who, 20 years ago, poured
scorn on the very idea of this type of scheme are now competing fiercely to
get a slice of the action. Soaring property values at Seaside have demonstrated
in the clearest possible terms that buyers will pay a large premium for a place
in this New Urbanist sun. The Emerald Coast, with its white sands and blue-
green sea, is now hot property and Seaside is used unashamedly by realtors as
an emblem of success. *Homes & Land of the Emerald Coast* is just one of several
property magazines that tell of the boom that has transformed this formerly
forgotten stretch of swamp and forest along the northern edge of the Gulf of
Mexico. Its pages carry pictures of well-groomed agents with television smiles
enticing potential buyers to invest through their particular company. In an
area where even a vacant plot of land can sell for more than a million dollars
there is a great deal at stake.

WaterColor: Seaside's younger, New Urbanist neighbour

Immediately to the west of Seaside and in an arc around its northern edge is WaterColor, the largest example of a competing New Urbanist scheme. Extending over nearly 500 acres (compared with Seaside's 80) this is a corporate venture headed by the powerful St. Joe Company. With massive land holdings in Florida, including the present site that it has owned since 1927, the St. Joe Company has diversified from its original base of forestry and paper production to real estate development. As well as WaterColor, the company is also developing a smaller project of this kind, WaterSound Beach, along the same stretch of coast.

WaterColor has been developed over a much shorter period than Seaside and to a unified design shaped by architect Jacquelin Robertson (who had previously worked on the master-plan for the Disney model settlement, Celebration); as a result there is less diversity than in Seaside and little scope for spontaneity. Everything in WaterColor is as near perfect as one could imagine. The buildings are carefully proportioned and exquisitely colour matched, and the communal spaces are meticulously maintained; so too are the paving slabs along the sidewalks and the roads themselves. It has been designed wholly as a resort community and all the support facilities are there to provide a perfect vacation in a Southern landscape. The WaterColor Inn offers luxurious accommodation facing the beach and this is supplemented by a wide choice of rental properties dotted about the town. At the end of a day on the beach, or spent canoeing across the community's own lake, sun-kissed diners make their way to the prestigious Fish out of Water dune-side restaurant. It's all very wonderful but this very perfection leaves one missing the untidiness around

In so many ways, Seaside is recognised as a striking exemplar of what modern planning in the US ought to be

some of the Seaside houses, the sandy paths that merge with the adjoining gardens, and the informal dining outlets along the downtown frontage. Seaside has the vivacity of a child's painting; WaterColor is painting by numbers.

Further down the coast, to the east of Seaside and WaterColor, is another new settlement in the same lineage, Rosemary Beach. Dating from 1995 and designed by Duany and Plater-Zyberk this, too, is a strongly themed development; the style of architecture is modelled on traditional, small waterfront towns of the Caribbean. It is a beautifully crafted place, displaying the familiar New Urbanist elements of human scale (the whole site is slightly larger than Seaside), inter-weaving lanes and footpaths, and central services within walking distance of every home. The architecture, which bears traces of earlier Dutch and Spanish colonial influence in the Caribbean, is matched to its climate and marine location with high ceilings and open balconies to allow sea breezes to circulate in the living areas. Stronger colours are used as well as pastels, and traditional building materials are always favoured; learning from the experience of Seaside, where the houses need to be regularly repainted, here the requirement is for wood to be stained at the time of construction, allowing the buildings to grow old gracefully. Property values, at least as high as anywhere along Highway 30A, tell their own story of consumer assent.

Apart from these localised examples, there is plentiful evidence from elsewhere that New Urbanism is making its mark and that Seaside is cited as an important model. Nationally in the United States and internationally, Seaside has been widely acclaimed for breaking a depressing tradition of decades of appalling design in American settlements. The architects Christopher Alexander and Jenny Quillien highlight one achievement in particular, namely that Duany and Plater-Zyberk have discovered a way (through the use of design codes) to exercise control and consistency in large developments without personally designing individual buildings. Referring specifically to Seaside, they conclude that the outcome is 'a humane environment, pleasant, avoiding many of the mishaps and ugliness of modern American development. It has charm.'[16]

In order to promote the principles of this approach to new development, the Seaside Institute has been formed in the heart of the pioneer settlement. It is dedicated to 'promoting the building of community in cities and towns through design, education and the arts'. Phyllis Bleiweis is the Institute's Executive Director and tells of some 400 New Urbanist projects across the United States, as well as a growing list elsewhere. On account of the working example on its doorstep, the Institute is at the forefront of the debate on sustainability and restoration of civic life in American towns and cities. It not only hosts events in Seaside but, through a series of organised seminars, works tirelessly to talk to civic leaders in other locations. It has also spawned an

'Truman House' is a reminder of when Seaside itself was used as a film set

offshoot in Italy, the Seaside Pienza Institute for Town Building and Land Stewardship, which in 2004 located its annual gathering in the UK and included Poundbury in its programme of visits. Inevitably, a meeting with the Prince of Wales was a highlight of the programme.

Of course, Seaside and the whole New Urbanist agenda also has its critics. For many, a visit to Seaside seems like stepping back in time, and, enjoyable though that may be, it is seen as a rejection of the full potential of modernity and, indeed, of reality itself. From this perspective it can be likened to a film set of the past, a point that was made forcefully by its selection for 'The Truman Show', a film in which Jim Carrey's character plays out his life on the stage of an idealised small town community, unaware of the way in which he is contained and manipulated. While the film gave publicity to the project (and also a valuable source of income that enabled the building of the town school) it was inevitable that it would also encourage a view that it is a make-believe world for the very rich to indulge their fantasies.

Similar one-dimensional criticism has also been directed to Poundbury and must be regarded as part and parcel of any innovative attempt to break the mould.

The fact remains that observations are overwhelmingly favourable. Don't be misled, exhorted one defender of the concept: 'you could be forgiven for thinking it's about nostalgia and cliché. Actually, Seaside is an incredibly diverse assembly of contemporary buildings.'[17] *Time* magazine anticipated that it could become 'the most astounding design achievement of its era, and one might hope, the most influential'.[18] Or as *Newsweek* commented: 'Seaside – with its cozy, narrow streets, its jumble of pastel-colored homes – is probably the most influential resort community since Versailles.'[19]

Notes

1   John Thompson, 'New Urbanism – friend or foe?', *Town & Country Planning*, Vol. 74, No. 1, January 2005, pp.20-21
2   Robert Davis, in Brooke (1995), p.17
3   Prince of Wales (1989), p.144
4   Christopher Alexander and Jenny Quillien, 'The vital work of Andres Duany: a commentary', http://www.patternlanguage.com/townplanning/duany.htm
5   I have made extensive use of Steven Brooke's excellent and beautifully photographed account of Seaside, in his book of that name, Brooke (1995)
6   Alexander and Quillien, *op. cit.*
7   Prince of Wales (1989), p.143
8   American song-writer, Bob DePiero, who has a second home in Seaside: in 'Celebrated song-writer sings Seaside's praises', *Coastal Homes & Lifestyles*, Fourth Quarter 2004, pp.46-47
9   Brooke (1995), p.71
10 Mohney and Easterling, eds. (1991), p.66
11 Brooke (2003), p.10
12 *Executive Traveller*, June/July 2003, p.4
13 *Ibid.*, p.48
14 *Ibid.*, p.60
15 Prince of Wales (1989), p.146
16 Alexander and Quillien, *op. cit.*
17 David Lunts, Head of Urban Policy in the Office of the Deputy Prime Minister, in *The Guardian*, 12 May 2004
18 *Time*, January 1990
19 *Newsweek*, January 1995

Chapter 9

Back to the Future

'Overall, I reckon hats off to Charlie: he could have washed his hands of the land; instead he is trying to achieve something that, in a quaintly old-fashioned way, is truly radical.'[1]

L ike any project to create a new settlement, Poundbury is a brave undertaking. But it is little wonder that opinions are divided: building new communities is no mean task and the history of doing so is one of mixed fortunes. In this case, there is an added twist in the fact that it is the brainchild of the Prince of Wales and he is personally identified with its progress. In sifting through the record to date, one has to sort out valid criticism from mischievous anti-royalist barb.

Poundbury has been in the making for more than ten years. There is still more work to be undertaken to complete it than has been achieved to date and this could take at least another 15 years. But now is a good time to take stock of the 'Poundbury effect'. What is working well, and what could be done better?

Taking a wider view, what are some of the lessons for new developments elsewhere, and is Poundbury succeeding as a model of sustainability? More speculatively (considered in the final chapter), what will Poundbury be like in, say, another quarter century?

The Poundbury Effect: Breaking the Mould

'We don't want to suggest that it's the answer to all the world's housing problems, but we do suggest it is one solution to the modern problems of housing.'[2]

Poundbury is less than half way to completion but there is enough in place to weigh up the main *pros* and *cons*. Even the most prejudiced critic would find it hard to ignore some undoubted achievements in the development of Poundbury, notably, in urban design and architecture, in working towards sustainability, and in giving a start to a lively new community. From a purely commercial point of view, too, one can point to considerable success. In a comprehensive survey of reactions to Phase 1, the conclusion is that this experiment has worked out well for users and producers alike: 'an experiment which has indeed *broken the mould* of speculative development, by demonstrating that previous norms are not cast in stone but can be challenged with positive results for all concerned'.[3]

Urban Design and Architecture

'I've seen the past and it works.'[4]

Perhaps the above quote is tempting fate, given that the original version, 'I've seen the future and it works', referring to the newly formed Soviet Union, proved to be hopelessly misjudged. The view (albeit with tongue in cheek) is worth recording, though, if only to acknowledge the juxtaposition of past, present and future that is at the intriguing core of Poundbury. Specifically, the new settlement deserves warm praise for important design and building features.

■ Leon Krier has provided a coherent master-plan that really does offer an effective framework for development. There are striking features in the plan that include a sharp edge between town and country, variety in the street scene, a balance between the demands of the car and those of pedestrians, the siting of signature buildings and the use of squares and monumental features. Historically, the urban designer *par excellence*, Camillo Sitte, inspired by some of the great cities of central Europe that he knew so well, could not have done better.

Poundbury is greatly valued for its exemplary urban design and architecture

■ The hierarchy of building codes has ensured that there is consistency from the master-plan through to individual building details, and even (in the form of guidelines) to anticipated changes by owners. As a planning process this represents an enormous achievement, demonstrating an unusual degree of flexibility and understanding, allowing variations around a common theme.

■ The design of individual buildings is of a very high standard. Adoption of a neo-traditional style is by no means to everyone's taste but all can be agreed that here is a conscious attempt to create a humane environment in a form that people actually want. Modernist architects will argue that a genuine choice has been denied and that there are attractive alternatives to traditional styles. That is true enough, but Poundbury was conceived in the wake of a miserable record of decades of schemes that range from indifferent to bad; against that background it was surely time to try an entirely fresh tack.

■ Building materials are also of a very high quality. Use has been made where possible of local materials, including recycled stone and architectural salvage. Although there is a cost premium attached to these there is clear evidence that buyers are prepared to pay the difference. Quality comes at a price but, in this case, at a price that the market is willing to meet.

■ The relative absence of street signs and urban clutter is a major achievement. The Poundbury street scene is not simply unique; it also offers a working model of what could quite easily be replicated elsewhere.

■ Overall, Poundbury has charm, despised by critics as a chocolate box representation of an imagined past but enjoyed by those who live there for its humanity and warmth. This is not a stage set of a yesteryear market town but an amenable setting for modern life in its various forms: 'a modern place that looks traditional'.[5]

In the words of one external observer: 'Poundbury is a pleasing amalgam of materials, styles and intimate scale ... among the town's most successful features is the architectural mix achieved by a well thought out set of guidelines that allows for variation and contrast.'[6]

Sustainability

'By raising the environmental standards of new housing, a major contribution can also be made to the overall quality of people's lives.'[7]

A second area of achievement lies in the pursuit of sustainability. This is not an easy concept to demonstrate as, if the truth be told, no modern development can really be sustainable. Poundbury, like anywhere else, has a voracious appetite for resources, but at least a conscious effort has been made to contain it where possible. Sustainability is now at the top of everyone's agenda and to find an experiment where its principles are enthusiastically championed is certainly worth recognition. Particular success can be claimed in three areas: building specifications, use of land, and traffic generation.

Individual buildings not only meet government sustainability specifications but in many cases go well beyond them. Some houses have been built deliberately with ecological innovation in mind.

The new settlement makes effective use of land, with an eventual population of more than 5000 on a site of 400 acres (a density of 20 per acre if one excludes 150 acres of open land); this compares well with the kind of conventional suburban development that has become the norm over past decades.

The location of open spaces around the edge (most evident at this stage on the southern periphery) provides a green transition to the surrounding countryside. There has been criticism that new development is edging out too far, especially to the south towards Maiden Castle, but overall there is a greater degree of sensitivity about the town-country boundary than one normally finds.

Finally, the whole development has been designed to encourage less use of the private car. Each of the four quarters of Poundbury will take no more than ten minutes to cross, which means that the proposed town centre, in a central location, will be within ten minutes of every household. Although only a small minority of the present population currently works within Poundbury it is planned to increase the proportion as development proceeds, and the hope is that people will choose to walk to work.

Community

'It's getting back to the basics of the community which seems to me to be essential if we are going to cut this tiny island up with many more houses.' [8]

Thirdly, as a measure of success, one can point to the unusual strength of community organisation and activities after just ten years of development. This can be evidenced in terms of the lively focus of Pummery Square and the varied use that is made of Brownsword Hall, the strength of self-management groups and, not least of all, the attempt to create a balanced town through its range of land uses and the social mix of people who live there.

For most of the first decade, Phase 1 residents missed the opportunity to buy groceries and newspapers from a local shop, to drop in somewhere for a coffee or visit their own pub. All of these gaps have now been filled and

Pummery Square is a lively focus for the community. As well as the permanent 'village shop' there are also regular farmers' markets, which have proved to be very popular.

Pummery Square is also home to Brownsword Hall, venue for a wide range of activities from dance classes to craft fairs, auction events to meetings of the Poundbury Ladies, table tennis competitions to pot luck suppers. It is managed by an elected committee, which also has responsibility for the use of the square itself.

From the outset there has been an effective Residents Association, acting not only as an important link between individuals but as a formal means of communication with the Duchy. In Poundbury's pioneering days, at a time when it is still developing, this has proved to be an important body. There are

also two management companies, formed by election of local residents, and these, too, are proving effective.

Above all, the whole point of Poundbury was to create not just another bland housing estate but a thriving community of a sort that one might find in a small market town. Not only does Poundbury look like such a place but it can point to a genuine mix of land uses – industry and offices as well as housing and shops – and a population drawn from across a wide social spectrum. As such, it compares favourably with other New Urbanist experiments elsewhere, especially those in the United States, which have been largely confined to private residential uses.

There is a strong sense of community, expressed in various ways

Commercial Achievement

*'At a simple level it is obvious that the fact that the sites were
bought at something very close to an agricultural price and that
the process of development has enormously enhanced this value,
implies that the investment must have been worthwhile financially.'* [9]

Garden cities and new towns have generally represented a good investment, not least of all because of the point about rising land values that Colin Ward makes (in relation to Britain's new towns) in the above quote. In contrast, other ideal schemes have failed to get off the drawing board because of a lack of commercial understanding. Poundbury was always going to be on sounder ground because, although the Prince and his master-planner might at times have wanted to follow a more utopian path, the Duchy (with the Treasury in

Local businesses are doing well as the population of Poundbury increases

the background) has retained a wary eye on its commercial viability. The fact that development has proceeded to plan is evidence of the balancing influence of the latter.

■ Figures are not readily available but there is every sign that this has proved to be a successful financial venture for the Duchy. The sale alone of 250 acres of building land (and another 150 acres for leisure uses) will have been the bedrock of this venture. Even allowing for the Duchy's own investments in the infrastructure and costs of guiding the scheme the balance will be well in favour of profitability. The Duchy is also in the enviable position of being able to release land as the market dictates without (in contrast to a more typical development project) ongoing liabilities for loan repayments.

■ There is also a continuing source of rental income, mainly through the industrial properties, in all of which the Duchy retains freehold possession.

In spite of early scepticism, Poundbury has also proved commercially attractive for house-builders, and national as well as local developers now compete for new tenders. Concerns that housing might not sell easily because of the presence of a nearby factory or social housing have proved to be largely unfounded.

The Poundbury Effect: Missing Links

'Not in Utopia ... but in this very world, which is the world of all of us – the place where in the end we find our happiness, or not at all!'[10]

Poundbury's achievements are very significant – in fact, quite remarkable in the short period since its inception – but it would be unrealistic to expect (or even to want) a place without imperfections. A true utopia would not only be impossible but also remarkably boring. Imperfections should be seen, instead, not so much as a mark of failure but as opportunities to learn from experience. If Poundbury is to provide an enduring model there are various issues that will call for further discussion, such as the question of density, neighbourhood rules, reconciling different tenure needs, the perennial problem of containing the car, community governance and working with local authorities. Most of the problems that arise are not insoluble, although some call for more radical solutions than others.

A Question of Density

'It feels as if the developers are hiding behind the rhetoric of Poundbury as an experiment to maximise their return ... now the ideology is taking a back seat to make money.'[11]

Relatively high densities are integral to the master-plan for Poundbury. People should be aware of this when they sign up to a place in the community. At the same time, developers should not see it as a blank cheque to do as they wish. Density is a contentious issue and the Duchy will need to acknowledge perfectly understandable concerns as well as to re-affirm the sound principles that guide the plans. High-density development requires a fine balancing act between different ideals, and like any balancing act will only be completed

Aerial view showing the steady expansion of Poundbury across the development site
(Courtesy: Duchy of Cornwall)

successfully if there is the utmost concentration and attention to detail. If future mistakes are to be avoided there are certain things to be done.

▪ Problems of over-looking have been avoided where possible but there are still examples of where this occurs. Detailed design is all-important in future planning. Likewise, at the detailed planning level, every attempt should be made to safeguard natural daylight for the small gardens and to yield as many hours of sunlight as possible.

▪ People will be more likely to accept high densities if the quality of development is also high, with an interesting mix of building materials and finishings as well as imaginative pockets of planting. There is generally a good record of success but also scope for localised improvements, especially in relation to more inventive uses of street and courtyard planting. The recent development of Whitecross Square is an example of a lost opportunity to create a civic focus.

▪ Many of the houses front directly onto the pavement and this is not to everyone's liking. Arthur Cole is a retired architect living in Poundbury who

High densities need to be carefully planned and managed to create an acceptable environment

argues that all houses should have a strip of 'defensible space', perhaps no more than two or three metres in depth, to protect people's privacy. He is also critical of 'non-defensible' space in the alleys and courtyards and fears that this may be a source of future problems.

▨ The policy of allowing subsequent house extensions needs to be re-visited. Plots are already very small and continuing to allow further extensions will inevitably reduce the enjoyment of neighbouring householders. The Duchy insists that external walls be raised when these are built but this can sometimes lead to an increased sense of containment for others.

▨ Provision of open spaces and other facilities, even if around rather than within the main housing areas, will need to keep pace with the continuing intensity of development. In the interests of biodiversity, quiet areas of natural vegetation will be of great value as well as organised play-spaces, and it is not clear, at this stage, if sufficient attention is being paid to the former. It might be timely to re-visit Poundbury's landscape plan to see if more can be done in the interests of both aesthetics and biodiversity.

Neighbourhood Rules

'When the wind is in the North
Sprigg's wireless bellows forth,
When the wind is in the West
Brigg's bonfire smoulders best.'[12]

Recognition has been made of the various links in the design and building chain but a final connection is missing. All householders receive in their

The Prince has always wanted Poundbury to be an attractive feature rather than a blot on the Dorset landscape

arrival pack a copy of the Poundbury Stipulations, a common-sense code designed to encourage good neighbourliness and to safeguard the local environment. This is a commendable document in itself (although by no means universally popular) but it carries little weight in the community.

For a start, householders who might have an issue to raise are frequently not clear about which body is the guardian of the Stipulations: is it the Duchy, or one of the management companies, or the Residents Association? Moreover, apart from residents who raise issues on their own initiative, there is no obvious mechanism to monitor where standards may be slipping. There are numerous instances of where the terms of the Stipulations are flouted (not always wilfully): un-neighbourly car parking, commercial vehicles parked in private spaces, and bin bags piled up in the streets well before collection times. Or, in other instances, there are particular pockets in the wind-swept town where litter perennially gathers; and some of the courtyards are used for noisy ball-games. Most infringements are quite minor in themselves but are just the kind of thing that can soon amount to local nuisance; and over time will lead, inevitably, to the deterioration of the carefully planned environment.

The problem is there but it is also one that can be easily resolved; a number of simple measures can be taken.

■ There needs to be a clear 'one stop' route for residents to direct issues and, equally, a clear response process. Clarify to all residents who it is that 'owns' the Stipulations and give a telephone number and email address to make contact simple; an early reporting of issues can help to nip things in the bud. The idea of service standards might seem needlessly formal but, as Poundbury grows and informal contact with the Duchy Office becomes less practical, something along these lines would be helpful.

▨ Re-visit the Stipulations regularly through public debate and consultation to ensure that they have widespread community support. What are the issues that really need to be kept under surveillance?

▨ Consider the appointment of a Poundbury Neighbourhood Officer to walk the patch and get to know residents on a personal basis. This could well be a part-time job, ideally for someone who lives in the community. Issues can be spotted as they arise and duties could include such practical tasks as extra litter clearing and reporting where repairs are needed. Such a post could be funded on the basis of an annual levy per household and implemented through the management companies. Good neighbourliness is not something that can necessarily be taken for granted; a little lubrication is needed to oil the wheels.

Social Conundrum

*'Both Poundbury and Bournville currently lacked a governance mechanism
that spanned tenure types. In both areas, there appeared to be a
sense of division between owner-occupiers and tenants.'* [13]

There is no easy answer to the contemporary challenge of how best to provide social housing. Monolithic council housing estates in the past have not worked (although that is at least in part a management rather than a planning issue) but 'pepper potting', as in Poundbury, is also not without its problems. The inclusion of social housing is a bold element of the overall plan and it generally works well, but there needs to be early recognition of where it works less well and, in consequence, how it can be improved.

For the tenants of social housing there is some evidence of resentment and an 'us and them' culture. Many of the tenants know that they will never be able to afford to buy a house in Poundbury, yet they witness on a daily basis the trappings of better-off neighbours with expensive cars and well stocked gardens. This proximity of a different lifestyle can be at best irritating and at worst hurtful. In turn, owner-occupiers comment on untidy rear gardens, on commercial vans and small trucks in the courtyards and open car parks, and on intrusive car maintenance being carried out (against the neighbourhood code) in the yards. None of these might seem of much importance to an outsider but they are enough to give rise to a degree of friction. Recognition of this type of issue would be the first step towards finding perfectly realistic solutions. The following are examples of what might be done.

▨ Apply the Poundbury Stipulations consistently and fairly to all occupants, whether owner-occupiers or social housing tenants. Where anti-social behaviour occurs it should be dealt with as an infringement in itself, regardless of where it originates.

▨ Provide every opportunity for tenants to buy their own property, on the obvious grounds that owners are more likely to invest in their homes and gardens than occupants on a limited tenure. There is already a variety of schemes on offer and these should be increased.

▨ Garages should be provided for social housing just as they are in houses to buy, partly to keep more cars out of public areas but also to offer the advantage of additional storage. Too often, through no fault of the occupier, a lack of storage space leads to untidy piles of materials in back gardens.

▨ A few well-screened car parks should be dotted around Poundbury to enable overnight parking for trade vehicles that currently have to be left in the street. Such car parks could double up as daytime parking areas for commercial premises.

▨ The landlord of social housing should include the planting of trees and shrubs in rear gardens at the time of occupation. This would immediately (and at low cost) put the appearance of social housing gardens on a par with those of owner-occupiers.

Living with the Car

'Will we, in the 21st century, escape from the 20th century motor age?' [14]

The Poundbury master-plan has made every attempt to reduce the number of car journeys in the town, and the Residents Association is constantly trying to encourage car owners to park in their own drives and garages rather than on the roads. In spite of these good efforts, there are still examples of bad practice.

▨ There is not a frequent, low-cost bus service from Poundbury to the centre of Dorchester. Not everyone is in a position to walk into town and back with bags of shopping, so as a result it is common to use one's own car. There is undoubtedly scope to reduce car journeys through the introduction of a good bus service; as the population of Poundbury grows this will become increasingly viable.

▪ Particularly as homes front directly onto the pavement, with at most a narrow front garden, aspects from the houses would undoubtedly be improved if there were less on-street parking. The Stipulations require that cars should be parked within one's own property or courtyard and there is clearly a need for this issue to be discussed by residents.

▪ Many residents also complain about the daily overspill of car parking from local firms. Industrial premises tend to have sufficient car parking spaces within their own enclosures but offices are not always so well provided; future planning permissions need to strike a balance between encouraging more employees to walk or use public transport and ensuring that there is at least a minimum allocation of dedicated space for parking.

Community Governance

'There has been strong encouragement for the development of local councils, i.e. town and parish councils, with an extended range of functions and roles.'[15]

Poundbury is well endowed with a high calibre of official and voluntary labour, with a strong commitment to making the place work. There are, however, basic structural weaknesses that are already evident. The situation of who does what is confusing. Within Poundbury there are the builders, who retain responsibility for various operational matters (including street lighting) prior to a formal hand-over; there is the Duchy, with its overall brief but also with a continuing involvement in some operational issues; there are two management companies, one for the first phase and one for the second; and an active Residents Association. Then there are a number of external authorities – the Regional Assembly, County Council, District Council and Town Council, each of the last three with elected representatives. These are early days but unless the situation is simplified (as, for example, suggested below) it will pose a significant threat to effective community governance – more than that, without this it will become increasingly difficult to prevent important elements of the Poundbury vision from unravelling.

▪ Form a single Poundbury Management Executive, with representatives from the Duchy, the present management companies, the Residents

Association, business interests and local authorities. The main task of the Executive would be to provide a common voice on matters of general concern and to safeguard the essential principles and qualities of Poundbury.

■ Each of the member organisations would also operate locally in each of the three or four neighbourhoods that will emerge as the development nears completion. Neighbourhoods with 1500 or so residents in each would be meaningful as well as manageable.

■ Include in the planned town square a small building equivalent to a French *mairie* to house the various interests dedicated to an authentic model of government at the most local level.

Working with Local Authorities

'A local government officer
Is seldom a philosopher,
Nor will he often go so far
As to express ideals;
But in affairs municipal
He is a man of principle,
Inflexible, invincible.'[16]

There was always the potential for a difficult relationship with the local authorities, simply on account of the experimental nature of Poundbury and the intention to break with convention. In the event, potential difficulties have generally been minimised and there is a progressive attitude to Poundbury's ideals. Some aspects in particular, highways being the obvious example, are more restricted by inflexible regulations than others. An over-cautious policy to provide a sufficient number of car parking spaces, for instance, has in some cases led to a sacrifice of roadside tree planting in favour of extra parking bays. More strikingly, the appearance of Poundbury's roundabouts is hardly uplifting. As focal points in the town, one might have expected something more imaginative, perhaps with exhibits of sculpture or a fountain. Instead, the roundabouts are largely barren circles with an excess number of traffic warning signs. Surely a great opportunity for more public art has been missed.

As well as such examples, there is also a tendency for some councillors to see Poundbury as a privileged place that needs to be taken down a notch or two. There was, for example, more than an element of mischief in a proposal to locate a recycling plant in Poundbury, ignoring the fact that this must be one of the most wind-blown sites for miles around.

It must be hoped that over time local antagonism will become a thing of the past. To avoid needless friction and to enable all aspects of the new development to meet the high standards of its designers, the following is suggested.

▨ Poundbury should be given delegated planning, highways and waste management powers so that it can be directly responsible for aspects of its own local environment. Funds would be raised as a proportion of the council tax.

▨ It would elect its own dedicated councillors, who would serve on the District Council, representing the interests of Poundbury but also contributing to the wider government of West Dorset. This would give Poundbury a stronger local voice without leading to an artificial separation.

▨ Consider the creation of Poundbury's own Town Council. If it remains part of the Dorchester Town Council the latter will be responsible for a population of more than 20,000 – surely too many for what is really intended as the equivalent of a traditional parish council.

Model for the Future?

'I am here at the invitation of The Prince to look at Poundbury, which in many respects is a model of what the Government is trying to achieve.' [17]

Britain is not alone in embarking on a major programme of house-building, in response less to a gross increase in population than to an unmet demand for greater flexibility in provision. A 'one size fits all' approach to housing is no longer enough in the face of a much wider diversity of households, from first-time buyers to down-scaling retirees. In this ongoing context of social change the opportunity to look first-hand at an experiment like Poundbury is invaluable. It may not have all the answers but it would be rash to ignore the experience and to ask what it can tell us about planning future settlements. As a possible model for others, not for replication but as a source of principles, the experience of Poundbury suggests a number of important elements that may be essential if a scheme is going to go beyond convention: inspirational leadership, planning at all levels, attention to detail, good stewardship and freedom to experiment.

Inspirational Leadership

The Prince of Wales at an event to mark the tenth anniversary of Poundbury (Courtesy: Duchy of Cornwall)

The most successful new communities reflect the vision and leadership of a committed sponsor. In the first chapter, historical examples were shown, such as Bournville and Port Sunlight, Letchworth and Welwyn; these were all conceived and strongly promoted by individuals, albeit later with the support of dedicated organisations. In the comparative study of Seaside in the United States, there, too, it was a benevolent developer who had both the vision and means to break the mould of conventional real estate practice. With Poundbury, it would be impossible to think of its progress without the persistent interest and ideas of the Prince of Wales. The vision is his but so, too, is the land; more than that, he has almost certainly been able to make some things happen that would not have been possible without him. More generally, model settlements for the future are most unlikely to be created through committees and, experience would suggest, ideally not through local or central government agencies.

Planning at All Levels

A second lesson is that it is one thing to have a vision but quite another to know how to translate it into reality. A most important lesson from the experience of Poundbury is that a means was developed to link the vision to a coherent master-plan and then through further stages to implementation; moreover, the essential principles of the master-plan are maintained by means of continuing controls after buildings pass into the hands of individual owners. Planners of future settlements would do well to take account of this use of a hierarchy of plans and codes, which is one of the most telling features in the making of Poundbury.

Some attempts have already been made to borrow a leaf from the Poundbury book. With its close experience of this experiment, West Dorset District Council has become something of a champion of good-quality, high-density development. Even before Poundbury, it had won a commendation from the Royal Town Planning Institute for a mixed-tenure housing scheme in the nearby village of Abbotsbury, and is currently supporting a 500-house extension of Charlton Down, another village on its patch. David Evans, the Director of Planning and Environment, has identified ten key principles from the experience of Poundbury that may also be relevant to other authorities.

He points to *site selection*, which some might question given Poundbury's exposure to heavy winds and rain from the south-west; and then a *bold urban design framework*, of the sort that Leon Krier has provided so effectively; *permeability*, meaning integrated settlements with a choice of ways of getting from one part to another; *legibility*, derived from a hierarchy of routes and landmark features; *vitality*, with houses fronting directly onto streets and squares; a *mix of uses*, with factories and workshops located before new housing to enable residents to make informed decisions; *affordable housing* dispersed amongst non-subsidised homes and built to appear indistinguishable; *identity*, achieved through a design code; *enclosure*, with streets designed flexibly to allow for the car without being dominated; and *implementation*, with effective use of Section 106 agreements to secure maximum social benefit. One can look critically at some or all of these principles, but the idea of developing a consistent approach to what amounts to a new style of urban development cannot be questioned. If high-density, sustainable schemes represent the future for planning, this attempt to codify and learn from experience is to be welcomed.[18]

Detail Matters

Following on from a hierarchy of plans and codes, an important lesson from Poundbury is that detail really does matter. The integrity of a concept depends to a considerable degree on the quality and effectiveness of local stewardship. Even the best-laid plans will come to naught if controls are relinquished too early in the process. In part, this is an ideological issue and there is a strong body of opinion that would resist too much control over people's lives. The opposing view is that controls can be justified if they help to protect the interests of the wider community and if those who are subject to them choose to be so. When people buy into Poundbury they are aware at the outset that they can only paint their front doors from a limited palette, that they are not allowed to park a boat or caravan in public view, and that plans for even a garden shed are subject to Duchy approval. Such restrictions are too much for some to bear, but for others the price is well worth paying to uphold standards for the whole community. If there is a criticism of Poundbury in this respect it is that there is not too much control over detail but still too little. This is an important lesson to bear in mind in subsequent schemes.

Freedom to Experiment

Finally, it is clear that even the heir to the throne cannot easily overcome the constraints imposed by the very planning, highway and building regulations that were originally designed to lead to better conditions in our towns and cities. Over time, the system has become exceedingly bureaucratic and the rigidity of procedures too often stands in the way of experimentation. Concessions have been made to allow Poundbury to go ahead, and ways have been found to circumvent obstacles, but the long arm of officialdom combined with local politics has not proved to be a force for the good.

In an earlier study that I undertook with Colin Ward, we argued for the creation of *laisser faire* areas for housing, unencumbered by restrictions, that would be akin to the commercial enterprise zones favoured by Government in the 1980s. This concept could be extended to an innovative, mixed development scheme like Poundbury. In this case, it would enable the designation of the Duchy's 400 acres so that development would be subject only to minimal external rules that would leave the market as the main arbiter of what is built. In other words, no developer could afford to ignore the likes and dislikes of eventual buyers but at the same time it would be possible to offer something quite new. Buyers are seldom offered a real choice, but in what might be termed 'free development zones' that is exactly what they would find.

Experience to date should be used to assist in future development planning elsewhere. At the same time, Poundbury should not be seen as a panacea, nor should it be dismissed simply because it offends this or that architectural fashion or because it enjoys royal patronage. Faced with an almost overwhelming demand for new homes, this is the time for truly 21st century solutions: places that are sustainable while at the same time providing an environment with character; using the most advanced modern technologies yet not eschewing tradition; socially inclusive but not unrealistic in a reliance on social engineering; suitable for brownfield sites as well as green; in sympathy with existing settlements as well as creating something quite new. Poundbury is the first modern experiment of its kind and it is already something of a landmark. Just as Letchworth, more than a century ago, broke new ground and was to influence new communities across the world, it is probable that Poundbury will assume a similar role. It might be fitting, therefore, to conclude with the words of Ebenezer Howard, the founder of Letchworth, an inventor at heart who saw in every experiment an opportunity to progress:

> 'A successful invention or discovery is usually a slow growth, to which new elements are added, and from which old elements are removed, first in the thought of the inventor, and subsequently in an outward form, until at last precisely the right elements and no others are brought together. Indeed, it may be truly said that if you find a series of experiments continued through many years by many workers, there will eventually be the result for which so many have been industriously searching… [one] must profit by past experiences, and aim at retaining all the strong points without the weaknesses of former efforts.' [19]

Notes

1   Sophie Campbell, *Saturday Telegraph*, 28 June 2003
2   Simon Conibear, Press Release, 8 November 2004, http://www.princeofwales.gov.uk
3   Butina-Watson *et al.* (Report, 2004), p.41
4   Francis Golding, architectural consultant, in 'Prince's pet village gets seal of approval', *The Observer*, 14 May 2000
5   View of a resident, in Butina-Watson *et al.* (Report, 2004), p.17
6   Carolyn Torma, an American visitor to Poundbury, 'Prince Charles builds a new town', http://www.planningorg/thecommissioner/fall98
7   Ralph Rookwood, TCPA Vice-President, in TCPA (Report, 2003), p.5
8   Prince of Wales, 8 November 2004, http://www.princeofwales.gov.uk
9   Ward (1993), p.88
10   Ward (1974), p.114
11   David Dawkins, founding member of PROD, in 'Fear and loathing in Poundbury', *The Independent*, 26 August 2004
12   'Neighbourly Winds', in Osborn (1959), p.27
13   Martin Knox and David Alcock, 'Community governance for mixed tenure neighbourhoods', November 2002, http://www.jrf.org.uk
14   Ward (1991), p.109
15   Janice Morphet, 'The new localism', *Town & Country Planning*, Vol. 73, No. 10, October 2004, p.293
16   Osborn, 'Ballad of the Water-Butt of Altershutt', *op. cit., p.95*
17   Keith Hill, Minister for Housing and Planning, on a visit to Poundbury on 16 September 2004, http://www.princeofwales.gov.uk
18   David Evans, 'Positive planning - breaking the mould of new housing developments', *Planning*, No. 1549, 19 December 2003
19   Howard (1898), Chapter 9, 'Some difficulties considered'

Chapter 10

Poundbury 2030

'... it may be called a vision rather than a dream.'[1]

Six years ago the final brick was laid, just 30 years after the completion of Poundbury's first house. In keeping with the young town's love of celebration, the event was marked by a visit of the reigning monarch, whose idea this unique project was in the first place. Some of the pioneer residents recall how the noisy arrival of the then Prince's helicopter, landing on open ground to the south of the development, was a regular occurrence. The Prince took a keen interest in every stage of Poundbury's progress, from its beginnings as a dusty building site on a wind-swept hill to the settled community it is now, a small town in its own right. More recently, visits have become less frequent, in the face of his onerous duties of State, but a close bond remains between Charles and his brainchild.

Poundbury, not so long ago a mere gleam in the Prince's eye, is now well and truly on the map of England and continues to attract interest from around the world. Seeing the reality of a lively community, looking in every way like an historic town, it is hard to believe that when the project was first announced at the end of the 1980s there were many who said it would never be built. They were an odd alliance of Jeremiahs – so-called progressive architects, republicans and an almost universally sceptical press – but fortunately the Prince pursued his cause regardless. Over the years the voices of these doubters have rather faded, partly as a result of the striking evidence of successful completion, but also because their attention has been distracted by a new generation of experiments in other parts of the country. For one of the important outcomes of Poundbury is the way it broke the mould of a whole era of previous development, showing that it really is possible to build places that people will enjoy and which, at the same time, contribute to the inherent beauty of the English landscape. None of these later schemes is, quite rightly, a replica of Poundbury, but there is hardly a modern developer who has not adopted and helped to nurture at least some of the ground-breaking features of the pioneer settlement.

The contrast with an earlier generation of new towns is dramatic; unlike the post-1945 State-initiated new towns, Poundbury is weathering well, and by no means simply in a physical sense. Walking through the streets is a comfortable experience, and the picturesque architecture remains very much in vogue. It was a fascinating place when it was built, with a novel variety of building styles and appealing street scenes, and the passing of the years has not diminished this. Phase 1, completed after the first ten years, has consolidated itself as a village, just as the original inhabitants wanted, and the completion of the Poundbury Parkway (although opposed at the time) has helped to define its boundaries. Trees planted when it was built are now of a good height and spread and are much admired by visitors as well as residents. The second phase was never as coherent as the first and, with homes selling easily in the buoyant housing market of the early 2000s, there was a short period when standards tended to slip; the visitor, for instance, will see less use of attractive varieties of Dorset stone and rather too much of brick. Fortunately, these deficiencies were acknowledged, and more recent development is every bit as good as in the first phase, albeit at higher densities.

Gardens in Poundbury, as critics have always been quick to point out, are typically very small but, as if in defiance of these limits, residents have been prodigious in their planting. Trees and shrubs have now reached maturity and it is a delight to catch the fragrance of honeysuckle and clematis spilling over garden walls, and to see a profusion of foliage in the streets as well as on private plots. Flowers and herbs in the narrow front gardens were from the outset a striking feature and it is reassuring to see this tradition very much alive and well. People have adapted sensibly to the climate changes produced by global warming, and Mediterranean vegetation is ever more common. Another change can be seen in the spread of allotment gardens, once confined to a single site but now dotted around the green periphery. Organic food is no longer a mere fad and most households are keen for the chance to grow some of their own food supply; with the impact of astronomic fuel prices that became commonplace in the second decade of this century, it is also a cheaper option than buying vegetables brought in from elsewhere. There is also a little goat farm that is popular for its cheeses as well as a place for young children to visit.

Other features that were novel when they were introduced have not only stood the test of time but have also been widely adopted elsewhere. One is the idea of mixing land uses, with light industry and offices mingled amongst the housing. There were originally odd cases of friction, mainly to do with parking in front of private homes, but especially since the use of the car has lessened there is little evidence now of this former problem. Back in the first decade of the present century there was quite a furore over plans to site some heavy industry in Poundbury but these were later modified. Apart from that, most people accept the mixture of uses as part and parcel of town life and would find it hard to imagine why it used to be common to separate these in the first place.

The other novel feature was that of creating a genuine mix of tenures, to include affordable housing both to buy and rent. This was always more contentious and not to everyone's liking, in all tenures, but over time it has attracted less attention. Moves to increase the ratio of social housing to as much as 50 per cent were resisted and all seem agreed that the former yardstick of about one in three works well. Most of the early difficulties have been resolved and it is interesting to see how this kind of provision has become common elsewhere. Certainly, no-one would want to go back to the days of monolithic council estates.

Poundbury is still a popular venue for journalists and planning pundits but over the years attention has shifted away from the novelty of the townscape and more to the progress that has been made in governance. In the early days there was a profusion of agencies, all with a slice of responsibility for something, and it was uncertain what would happen when the Duchy took a lesser role. Fortunately, this challenge coincided with a growing disaffection nationally with the performance of local government and a recognition that reforms were needed not so much at a regional level (which was once conventional wisdom) but at the scale of local communities. The outcome was that Poundbury became one of the first places to pioneer a new style of localism, enjoying delegated powers that once rested at a higher level. Some people compare the outcome with the long-established French *commune*, with its own *mairie*, that one finds throughout that country and which provides a true community level of government. The advantages of this in Poundbury can be seen in the well-kept streets, litter free and lined with trees and flowers, and in the appointment of neighbourhood officers to keep a friendly eye on things on behalf of the rest of the community. These people are invariably colourful characters and each in their own way has added something indefinable to the quality of Poundbury life.

Needless to say, the vigour of community life that characterised the pioneering days is undiminished. Some feared that there might have been a waning of enthusiasm as time went on but, if anything, the opposite has been the case. With its greater maturity has come a more deeply embedded pattern of activities and co-operative ventures. Brownsword Hall still has a special place in the hearts of the earlier residents, but the opening of Elizabeth Hall (named in memory of the late Queen, Elizabeth II) is in every sense a focal point for the whole community. Its centrality means that it is within walking distance from every point and Leon Krier's high clock tower gives it a fitting sense of symbolism. With the completion of a variety of play areas around the edge of the settlement and the opening (after repeated delays) of a multi-purpose leisure centre, the younger generations are also much happier with what Poundbury has to offer than they seemed to be in the early days.

The long-awaited town centre, named, according to the then Prince's wishes, Queen Mother Square, was one of the last features to fall into place. True to an original promise to Dorchester, this was never planned to compete with the parent settlement but rather to concentrate on meeting some of the essential needs of the 5500 people who now live in Poundbury. This was, in any case, always going to be a symbolic as well as functional centre and Krier had long had his plans on the drawing board. As well as the iconic clock tower above Elizabeth Hall, the square is home to a fine statue of a Dorset peasant, inspired by no less than Thomas Hardy and recalling the kind of labourer who once would have toiled in the very fields on which Poundbury is built. The appearance of the square is also enhanced by various forms of public art and open-air exhibitions. Around the edge, the architecture is characterised by arches and a colonnade, attractive public seating and kiosks; it is a colourful scene and the people sitting at the tables and chairs of cafés and wine bars (renowned for the fine Dorset wines that offer at least some compensation for global warming) add to the noise and bustle.

Of course, there are those who still say that Poundbury is too 'twee' and contrived, but the fact remains that people who live there are generally more than satisfied with their surroundings, as they always have been. Poundbury residents will, at the same time, be the first to rebut claims that this is a utopia, for they will know best of all that although it really is very good it can never be perfect. Apart from the odd shortcomings in the built environment, the more important point is that one's happiness is not geographically bound and there will be as many personal difficulties to contend with in Poundbury as there are in any other place. But all are agreed that, as a place to live and work, this is at least as good a new settlement as any other and probably better than most. The King is known to be more than content with this outcome.

Note

1   Morris, 1890 (1970 edition), p.182

References

Books

Armytage, W.H.G. (1961) *Heavens Below: Utopian Experiments in England 1560-1960*. London: Routledge & Kegan Paul

Beevers, R. (1988) *The Garden City Utopia: A Critical Biography of Ebenezer Howard*. Basingstoke: Macmillan

Brooke, S. (1995) *Seaside*. Gretna, Louisiana: Pelican

Brooke, S. (2003) *Seaside Picket Fences*. Gretna, Louisiana: Pelican

Brown, J. (1999) *The Pursuit of Paradise: A Social History of Gardens and Gardening*. London: Harper Collins

Bryson, B. (1995) *Notes from a Small Island*. London: Doubleday

Burnett, J. (1978) *A Social History of Housing 1815-1970*. Newton Abbot: David & Charles

Coates, C. (2001) *Utopia Britannica: British Utopian Experiments 1325-1945*. London: Diggers & Dreamers Publications

Darley, G. (1975) *Villages of Vision*. London: Architectural Press

Draper, J. (2001) *Dorchester Past*. Chichester: Phillimore

Economakis, R., ed. (1992) *Leon Krier: Architecture and Design 1967-1992*. London: Academy Editions

Fearnley-Whittingstall, J. (2002) *The Garden: An English Love Affair*. London: Seven Dials

Hardy, D. (1979) *Alternative Communities in Nineteenth Century England*. London: Longman

Hardy, D. (1991) *From New Towns to Green Politics*. London: Spon

Hardy, D. (2000) *Utopian England: Community Experiments 1900-1945*. London: Spon

Howard, E. (1898) *To-Morrow: A Peaceful Path to Real Reform*, reprinted in 2003 with commentary by Peter Hall, Dennis Hardy and Colin Ward. London: Routledge

Jackson, A.A. (1973) *Semi-Detached London*. London: Allen & Unwin

Krier, L. (1998) *Architecture: Choice or Fate*. Windsor: Papadakis

Kropotkin, P. (1899) *Fields, Factories and Workshops*. 1985 edition, Colin Ward, ed. London: Freedom Press

Leccese, M. and McCormick, K., eds. (2000) *Charter of the New Urbanism*. New York: McGraw-Hill

Marsh, J. (1982) *Back to the Land: The Pastoral Impulse in England from 1880 to 1914*. London: Quartet

Miller, M. (2002) *Letchworth: The First Garden City*. Chichester: Phillimore

Mohney, D. and Easterling, K., eds. (1991) *Seaside: Making a Town in America*. New York: Princeton Architectural Press

Morris, W. (1890) *News from Nowhere*. 1970 edition, J. Redmond, ed. London: Routledge & Kegan Paul

Neal, P., ed. (2003) *Urban Villages and the Making of Communities*. London: Spon

Nesmith, L. (2003) *Seaside Style*. New York: Rizzoli

Noel, A. (1999) *Great Little Gardens*. London: Frances Lincoln

Osborn, F.J. (1959) *Can Man Plan?* London: Harrap

Prince of Wales (1989) *A Vision of Britain: A Personal View of Architecture*. London: Doubleday

Quest-Ritson, C. (2003) *The English Garden: A Social History*. London: Penguin

Ravetz, A. (2001) *Council Housing and Culture: The History of a Social Experiment*. London: Routledge

Stephens, E. (2004) *Walking with Dinosaurs in Poundbury: A Geological Description of the Stone Houses*. Poundbury

Stewart, C. (1952) *A Prospect of Cities*. London: Longmans, Green & Co.

Uglow, J. (2004) *A Little History of Gardening*. London: Chatto & Windus

Ward, C. (1974) *Utopia*. Harmondsworth: Penguin

Ward, C. (1991) *Freedom to Go: After the Motor Age*. London: Freedom Press

Ward, C. (1993) *New Town, Home Town: The Lessons of Experience*. London: Calouste Gulbenkian

Ward, S.V. (1992) *The Garden City: Past, Present and Future*. London: Spon

Reports

Andrews, C.L. and Smith, W.R. (2005) *Challenging Perceptions: Case Studies of Dispersed and Mixed Tenure New Build Housing Developments*. Newbury: Sovereign Housing

Butina-Watson, G. *et al.* (October 2004) *Learning from Poundbury*. Second draft. Oxford Brookes University

Commission for Architecture and the Built Environment (April 2004) *The Development and Use of Design Codes in the UK: Literature Review*. Bartlett School of Planning: University College London.

Dorset County Council (2002) *Highway Guidance for Estate Roads*. Dorchester: Dorset County Council

Duchy of Cornwall (n.d.) *Poundbury Design Guidance*. Commissioned by the Duchy and written by Dr. Mervyn Miller. Poundbury: Duchy of Cornwall

HRH The Prince of Wales, *Annual Reviews*. Clarence House. See also http://www.princeofwales.gov.uk

Murrain, P. (2002) *Understand Urbanism and Get Off Its Back*. London: TCPA

TCPA (2003) *Building Sustainably: How to Plan and Construct New Housing for the 21st Century*. London: TCPA

TCPA (2004) *Biodiversity by Design: A Guide for Sustainable Communities*. London: TCPA

Wiltshire, R. and Crouch, D. (2001) *Sustaining the Plot: Communities, Gardens and Land Use*. London: TCPA

Newspaper Articles, Websites, Journals and Conference Papers

These are detailed in the respective notes at the end of each chapter.

Index